China's Climate Policy

I0867142

To understand China's climate change policy is not easy, as the country itself is a paradoxical actor in global climate political economy: it formerly took a very suspicious stand on the scientific certainty of climate change, but recently it has become a signatory and firm supporter of the Kyoto Protocol; it stubbornly refuses to accept any emission-cutting obligations, but has gradually taken the lead in developing renewable energies and carbon trading business; it accuses Western countries of hypocrisy and irresponsibility, but ironically maintains close cooperation with them on low-carbon projects; it fears climate mitigation commitments may hamper its economic growth, but meanwhile spends lavishly on the research and development of clean energy and other green technologies.

This book, unlike other research works which explain China's climate policy from pure economics or politics/foreign policy perspectives, provides a panoramic overview of China's climate-related regulations, laws, and policies as well as various government and non-government actors involved in climate politics. Through analyzing the political and socioeconomic factors that influence the world's largest carbon emitter's participation in the global collective actions against climate change, the book argues that, as a vast continental state with a mix of authoritarian politics and a quasi-liberalized market economy, China's climate policy process is fragmented and self-defensive, seemingly having little room for significant compromises or changes; yet in response to the mounting international pressures and energy security concerns and attracted by lucrative carbon businesses and clean energy market, the regime is showing better-than-expected flexibility and shrewdness in coping with the newly emerged challenges. Its future climate actions, whether effective or not, are vital, not only for the success of the global mitigation effort, but for China's own economic restructuring and sustainable development.

The book is a unique research monograph on the evolving domestic and foreign policies adopted by the Chinese government to tackle climate change challenges. It concludes that, instead of being motivated by concern about its vulnerability to climate change, China's climate-related policies have been mainly driven by its intense attention to energy security, business opportunities lying in emerging green industries, and consideration of its image in global climate politics.

CHEN Gang is Research Fellow at the East Asian Institute (EAI), National University of Singapore. Since joining the EAI in 2007, he has been tracing China's environmental and energy policies and publishing extensively on the sustainable development of China. His research papers have appeared in internationally refereed journals, such as *The International Spectator*, *China: An International Journal*, *The Chinese Journal of International Politics*, and *The Journal of East Asian Affairs*. He has also contributed a number of book chapters on China's environmental governance, natural disaster management, and climate change politics to edited volumes published by Routledge, Rowman & Littlefield, and other scholarly publishers. He constantly provides policy papers and consultancies to the Government of Singapore, and is frequently interviewed by media such as the *Wall Street Journal*, *The Economist*, the BBC, NHK, Channel NewsAsia, and the Xinhua News Agency.

China Policy Series
Series editor
Zheng Yongnian, China Policy Institute,
University of Nottingham, UK

1. **China and the New International Order**
   Edited by Wang Gungwu and Zheng Yongnian

2. **China's Opening Society**
   The non-state sector and governance
   Edited by Zheng Yongnian and Joseph Fewsmith

3. **Zhao Ziyang and China's Political Future**
   Edited by Guoguang Wu and Helen Lansdowne

4. **Hainan – State, Society, and Business in a Chinese Province**
   Kjeld Erik Brodsgaard

5. **Non-Governmental Organizations in China**
   The rise of dependent autonomy
   Yiyi Lu

6. **Power and Sustainability of the Chinese State**
   Edited by Keun Lee, Joon-Han Kim and Wing Thye Woo

7. **China's Information and Communications Technology Revolution**
   Social changes and state responses
   Edited by Xiaoling Zhang and Yongnian Zheng

8. **Socialist China, Capitalist China**
   Social tension and political adaptation under economic globalisation
   Edited by Guoguang Wu and Helen Lansdowne

9. **Environmental Activism in China**
   Lei Xei

10. **China's Rise in the World ICT Industry**
    Industrial strategies and the catch-up development model
    Lutao Ning

11. **China's Local Administration**
    Traditions and changes in the sub-national hierarchy
    Edited by Jae-Ho Chung and Tao-chiu Lam

12. **The Chinese Communist Party as Organizational Emperor**
Culture, reproduction and transformation
Zheng Yongian

13. **China's Trade Unions – How Autonomous Are They?**
Masaharu Hishida, Kazuko Kojima, Tomoaki Ishii and Jian Qiao

14. **Legitimating the Chinese Communist Party since Tiananmen**
A critical analysis of the stability discourse
Peter Sandby-Thomas

15. **China and International Relations**
The Chinese view and the contribution of Wang Gungwu
Zheng Yongnian

16. **The Challenge of Labour in China**
Strikes and the changing labour regime in global factories
Chris King-chi Chan

17. **The Impact of China's 1989 Tiananmen Massacre**
Edited by Jean-Philippe Béja

18. **The Institutional Dynamics of China's Great Transformation**
Edited by Xiaoming Huang

19. **Higher Education in Contemporary China**
Beyond expansion
Edited by W. John Morgan and Bin Wu

20. **China's Crisis Management**
Edited by Jae Ho Chung

21. **China Engages Global Governance**
A new world order in the making?
Gerald Chan, Pak K. Lee and Lai-Ha Chan

22. **Political Culture and Participation in Rural China**
Yang Zhong

23. **China's Soft Power and International Relations**
Hongyi Lai and Yiyi Lu

24. **China's Climate Policy**
CHEN Gang

China's Climate Policy

CHEN Gang

Routledge
Taylor & Francis Group
LONDON AND NEW YORK

First published 2012
by Routledge
2 Park Square, Milton Park, Abingdon, Oxfordshire, OX14 4RN

Simultaneously published in the USA and Canada
by Routledge
711 Third Avenue, New York, NY 10017
First issued in paperback 2014

Routledge is an imprint of the Taylor & Francis Group, an informa company

© 2012 CHEN Gang

The right of CHEN Gang to be identified as the author of this work has been asserted by him in accordance with the Copyright, Designs and Patents Act 1988.

All rights reserved. No part of this book may be reprinted or reproduced or utilised in any form or by any electronic, mechanical, or other means, now known or hereafter invented, including photocopying and recording, or in any information storage or retrieval system, without permission in writing from the publishers.

Trademark notice: Product or corporate names may be trademarks or registered trademarks, and are used only for identification and explanation without intent to infringe.

British Library Cataloguing in Publication Data
A catalogue record for this book is available from the British Library

Library of Congress Cataloging in Publication Data
Chen, Gang, 1976–
China's climate policy/Gang Chen.
p. cm.—(China policy series; 24)
Includes bibliographical references and index.
1. Environmental policy—China. 2. China—Politics and government—21st century. I. Title.
GE190.C6C44 2012
363.738'74610951—dc23 2011048070

ISBN 13: 978-0-415-59313-7 (hbk)
ISBN 13: 978-0-415-70520-2 (pbk)

Typeset in Times New Roman
by Book Now Ltd, London

Contents

Figures and tables

Figures

Tables

Acknowledgments

I am indebted to a number of people and organizations in the preparation of this book. Much of the information for the study was collected during my work as a full-time research fellow at the East Asian Institute (EAI), National University of Singapore. Without a specialized library with a massive collection of English and Chinese materials on China and other research facilities provided by the EAI, the completion of the manuscript would have become impossible. I benefited tremendously from the feedback of my EAI colleagues on the research subject, including Wang Gungwu, Zheng Yongnian, John Wong, Lye Liang Fook, Lam Peng Er, Yang Mu and Sarah Tong. My fieldtrip to Tianjin, China, which was fully funded by EAI, has helped me to better understand the low-carbon economy and eco-city planning in this Chinese port city through exchanges with local officials and academicians. Lian Wee Li, James Tan and Ng Hui Hoon provided me with much-needed administrative support.

I would also like to express my gratitude to the Lee Kuan Yew School of Public Policy (LKYSPP) in Singapore that sponsored some of my overseas study tours to China, Japan and India. My special thanks go to Huang Jing, Harold Teng, Surya Sethi, Daisuke Asano, Jasmin Kaur and Esther Yeoh at the LYKSPP. I have learnt a great deal from interviews and exchanges with officials from China's National Development and Reform Commission, Japan's Ministry of Economy, Trade and Industry, India's Planning Commission and Singapore's Ministry of National Development during my fieldwork in those countries.

I am grateful to the Routledge, one of the leading academic publishers in the world, for the excellent editorial work. In particular, I would appreciate Robert Langham, Lam Yong Ling, James Cooke and Andrea Platts for their indispensable assistance in producing this work and three anonymous reviewers for their pertinent comments and suggestions.

Introduction

In the context of climate change, a global issue that sovereign states have been grappling with for decades, China is probably the country that gets most attention in the region of East Asia and the world due to its dominant share of global carbon emissions and worrying annual increase in emissions. To understand China's climate change policy is not easy, as the country itself is a paradoxical actor in the global climate political economy: historically it took a very suspicious stand on the scientific certainty of climate change, but it finally became a signatory to and firm supporter of the Kyoto Protocol; it stubbornly refuses to accept any legally binding obligations to cut emissions, but is gradually taking the lead in developing renewable energies and carbon trading business; it accuses Western countries of hypocrisy and irresponsibility, but ironically maintains close cooperation with them on low-carbon projects; it fears climate mitigation commitments may hamper economic growth, but meanwhile spends most lavishly on the research and development of clean energy and other emission reduction technologies.

Early studies have shown that the climate change/global warming issue in China has been intimately linked with efforts to modernize the economy and the energy strategy employed to fuel that modernization (Hatch 2003: 45), but it may not be appropriate to simply portray China's climate policy process as just a component of its energy policy formulation since the climate issue is generally a global environmental issue in which more complicated factors such as transnational cooperation, national image, ecological protection, growing public awareness, and civil society's attitudes towards consumerism are closely involved. Elizabeth Economy (1997: 21) has observed that, besides inherent materialized motivations on energy and development, exchanges and collaborations with foreign specialist communities – as well as international aid from development agencies – measurably increased Chinese understanding of global environmental challenges like climate change and the range of response measures that they considered, and in some cases actually transformed the thinking of Chinese officials. Following the logic of interrelating the international climate change regime and China's domestic policy making, a number of literatures discussed the forces and constraints behind China's climate policy focusing on interests, sovereignty and prestige in the realm of foreign policy (Elizabeth 1998; Zhang 2003; Hatch

2003; Kobayashi 2003; Lewis 2007; Heggelund 2007; Yu 2008, etc.). From the diplomatic perspective, most of the abovementioned studies have regarded China's climate policy as being basically static due to its constant resistance to emission-reduction commitments in international climate talks. Such business-as-usual judgment is based primarily on the overgeneralization of China's policy-making process, which in the past two decades has undergone dramatic changes such as pluralization, decentralization, and fragmentization (Lampton 2001; Hao and Lin 2005) in a fast-changing international and domestic context. It is true that China's climate policy-making process to a large extent is still vertically organized, with core departments like the National Development and Reform Commission and the Ministry of Foreign Affairs having the last word on most related issues. However, when China is further marketized and integrated into the international system, the number and type of pressure groups involved in climate policy making will have expanded substantially with diversified players like other ministries, big business entities, media, local governments, non-governmental organizations (NGOs) and even individuals playing increasingly significant roles in the entire process. Cabinet ministries like the Ministry of Finance, the Ministry of Science and Technology and the Ministry of Environmental Protection as well as large energy state-owned enterprises (SOEs) have their own substantial stakes in climate-related policies. Meanwhile, the media, non-governmental organizations and think-tanks in China are exerting increasing influence on the climate policy process, and local authorities are becoming more active in vying to achieve favorable energy and environmental policies.

In a more pluralistic policy environment, Chinese decision makers have to perceive the climate change issue from various perspectives instead of the traditional antithetical angle that simply saw emission reduction as an obstacle to economic growth. Enviable windfalls from participation in the Clean Development Mechanism (CDM) and production of renewable energy and related equipment have convinced China to prefer the "no-regret" strategy that emphasizes mitigation actions which provide fringe benefits like profitability and employment to the country, regardless of whether or not the threat of climate change is real. Despite the country's enduring resistance to quantified emission-cutting commitments, China actually has been subtly adjusting its climate-related policy from time to time to reflect the dynamic interests of various domestic players and to respond to increasing international pressures. China's obstinate rejection of legally binding mitigation obligations may have contributed to the fiasco of the Copenhagen Climate Summit, but no one can glibly dismiss China's for-the-first-time promise of a 40–45 percent cut in carbon intensity by 2020 as being insignificant and business-as-usual.

This book, unlike much other research that tries to explain China's climate policy from pure economics or politics/foreign policy perspectives, systematically updates China's domestic and foreign policy making related to its response to the climate change issue, and provides a panoramic view of China's climate-related regulations, laws and policies as well as various government and non-government actors involved in the climate policy process. Through analyzing the political and socioeconomic factors that influence the world's largest carbon emitter's participation in global collective actions targeted on the mitigation and adaptation of climate change, the book contends that, as a vast continental state with a mix of authoritarian politics and a quasi-liberalized market economy, China's climate change policy is fragmented and self-defensive, seemingly leaving little room for significant compromises or changes. Yet, in response to rising international pressures and domestic energy security issues, and attracted by lucrative carbon businesses and a clean energy market, the regime shows some sort of better-than-expected flexibility and shrewdness in coping with the newly emerged challenges. Its future climate actions, whether or not effective, not only are vital for the success of the international joint effort against climate change, but may help adjust the direction in which the country's development is heading and underpin the long-term sustainability of its sizzling economy. This book is a unique research monograph on the evolving domestic and foreign policy adopted by the Chinese government to tackle climate change challenges. It tries to consider the issues from a balanced perspective, not only focusing on the regime's weakness and problems, but also its progress in turning the challenge into a kind of rare opportunity and impetus to make the development more sustainable.

The first chapter includes a detailed retrospect of China's diplomatic performances from the very beginning of international climate talks, with the Kyoto Protocol that China has been deeply involved in being the main focus. Chapter 2 discusses whether China's consistent position of not accepting any quantified emission cutting commitments is reprehensible in the context of international climate politics when the rising power is emitting much more carbon than before into the atmosphere and scientists are depicting a more depressing picture of global climate change. This chapter argues that being both a major culprit and victim in climate politics, China deserves credit for supporting the Kyoto Protocol and adjusting its stand to acclimatize itself to the changing situation, but given a bleak international climate outlook and China's alarming energy and emission trajectory, Chinese planners need to keep open the possibility of making larger concessions to ensure that Chinese emissions peak and then decline within two decades. Chapter 3, besides depicting the historical evolution of China's inter-agency mechanism on climate change, provides evidence to prove that, given the profound impact on a broad set of interest groups in the party-state, the climate-related policies are often the outcomes of bureaucratic politics and inter-agency competitions within the regime rather than reasoned debates. Inside a Chinese government, overwhelmed by the strategic priority of modernizing the economy, economic and energy departments have been playing a predominant role in shaping the country's climate policy, while environmental administration from the central to local is in an inferior position in the policy process. Chapter 4 analyzes an important but often-ignored economic motive behind China's participation in global climate politics: the country's enormous benefits from the CDM under the framework of the Kyoto Protocol. It studies how much China has materially benefited from the CDM and how it manages to become the largest beneficiary from such business. Besides the cost-benefit analysis, the author will also try to explain China's success from a political perspective, showing that strong government intervention and support will be vital for promoting such complicated environmental projects. By July 2011, China hosted about 45 percent of the world's CDM projects, which produced more than 63 percent of the world's total certified emission reductions (CERs) annually. Chapter 5 explains why China, as a latecomer to modernization, can be swiftly emerging as the world's clean energy powerhouse. With a detailed description of China's laws, regulations and other national policies aimed at incentivizing the use of new renewables like wind and solar power, it reveals that Chinese policy makers may have considered economic factors such as energy supply and jobs rather than environmental issues but, in practice, these no-regret policies have been functioning as efficient means to help the country slow down its greenhouse gas growth and gain competitive positions in the clean energy sector. Chapter 6 discusses two controversial renewable alternatives that can help China to meet growing power demand and bring down carbon emissions simultaneously. In a low-carbon electricity scenario, China is eager to formulate the world's most ambitious policies with enormous investment in place to foster aggressive construction of new hydropower and nuclear plants. Compared with other democracies, the authoritarian one-party regime in China faces much less resistance from civil society when pushing forward those hydropower and nuclear mammoths that may pose a potentially serious threat to local ecology. Chapter 7 considers whether China's effort to transform Tianjin, a manufacturing hub in northern China, into a model city in the development of low-carbon and circular economy was effective enough to help the country better manage local mitigation efforts based on regional industry make-up and local climate and socioeconomic factors and, therefore, to provide a replicable example for nationwide actions. Orientated as China's third growth pole parallel with Shanghai and Shenzhen, Tianjin differs from its peers in its special focus on environmental protection and energy conservation. Besides a string of local policies to encourage sectors of renewable energy and related equipment production, this chapter also examines the well-known China-Singapore Tianjin Eco-city Project to show whether China, equipped with the know-how obtained from foreign partners to build low-carbon cities in balance with nature, is capable of transforming the internationally popular concept of "eco-city" into successful local practices. Chapter 8 considers the limited but perceivable impact exerted by the emerging NGOs, mass media, online groups and opinion leaders outside the bureaucratic system, upon China's climate politics, in which internalization of norms and agenda setting are essential for the final policy outcome. In contrast to the high pressure approaches often adopted by their foreign peers to convey dissatisfaction and concerns, Chinese civic organizations are more prone to undertake low-key activities that do not challenge governmental positions on the climate change issue, and thus do not jeopardize their own legal existence under China's political context. Even so, with the help of new information and communication technologies (ICTs) and linking up with international environmental organizations, the role of NGOs and other civic forces as norm advocates and independent watchdogs in China's climate-policy process should not be underestimated, as promotion of information sharing and public consciousness may be equally effective in reinforcing the climate position of an emerging economy within a restricted civil society.

The book concludes that it is not self-evident that the current Chinese climate-related policies have been mainly motivated by the country's concern about its vulnerability to global climate change, which is still seen by the government as a somewhat remote issue. China's unique inter-agency bureaucratic structure on climate policy making – as well as the consistencies and variations identified in its climate-related policy formulation – have revealed that increasing consciousness about potential climate consequences can only partially explain China's shift towards more aggressive mitigation actions. As a developing country that has always put economic growth ahead of environmental protection, China has been, for years, authorizing the National Development and Reform Commission (NDRC), the economic planning and energy regulation agency, and the Ministry of Foreign Affairs to take charge of the climate-related policymaking instead of other more environmentally aware departments like the Ministry of Environmental Protection and the China Meteorological Administration. China's policy making on climate change is to a large extent driven by its intensive attention to energy security, business opportunities lying in emerging green industries and its international image in global climate politics. The country aspires to utilize climate change as a moral driving force to boost clean energy and other green sectors so as to serve the dual goals of cleaning up and finding new growth points for its economy in the aftershock of the global financial crisis. In future global climate talks, it remains unlikely that China will yield to international pressure and accept mandatory emission-cutting targets, but it will probably use voluntary carbon-intensive benchmarks in place of cap-and-tax obligations. Moreover, China will participate more frequently in other bilateral and multilateral diplomatic actions on climate change, aside from the UN-track climate talks, to enhance its international image and thus alleviate external pressures.

1 China's participation in global climate politics

The People's Republic of China's (PRC) attention to environmental issues from its foundation was triggered by and intertwined with its participation in international environmental regimes since the early 1970s. Its subsequent policy trend in the green area has been heavily influenced by the patterns of participation in various transnational talks and cooperation on the global environmental commons and the establishment of green norms in the international community. When the PRC replaced Taiwan (the Republic of China) to take a legitimate seat in the United Nations and improved relations with Western countries in 1971, it immediately faced an urgent demand to set up a special organization in preparation for the upcoming United Nations Conference on the Human Environment (UNCHE) in June 1972. In direct response to such an impending diplomatic requirement, a leading panel on environmental protection was established under the State Council in 1971, which became the predecessor of the future environmental department in China. Although China was an inactive participant of the UNCHE, such participation still marked the start of China's environmental diplomacy and domestic environmental governance in the modern sense. From then on, China started to play an increasingly active role in international environmental diplomacy, joining in with more international institutions and expanding bilateral and multilateral exchanges in the green area. Gradually, and especially after China's economy started to take off thanks to the reform and open-door policy in the 1980s, the international community had to acknowledge that China's participation is integral to the success of any significant global environmental accord and China is among the world's largest contributors to three of the most critical global environmental problems: biodiversity loss, climate change, and ozone depletion (Economy 1998: 265). Although China's response to these global environmental challenges had been overshadowed by such intransigent propositions in the realm of high politics as supremacy of national sovereignty, development-first for the Third World, and the industrialized/developing nations dichotomies, its recalcitrant negotiating positions were gradually softened by the external impact of international actors upon China's domestic political process and foreign policy making. New institutions and processes that favored the interests of environmentally proactive actors within China radically reconfigured the very nature of PRC environmental politics (Economy 1998: 265).

Constructing a response to ozone depletion and climate change

When China was showing stronger interest in engaging in both international and domestic environmental activities during the late 1980s and early 1990s, two critical environmental issues – ozone depletion and climate change – occupied the media headlines due to their potentially devastating threat to the ecosystem and humanity and, therefore, demanded global collective actions by each sovereign state. To avoid the Tragedy of Commons (Hardin 1968: 1243) and successfully provide the public benefits of ozone layer protection and mitigation of climate change, the international community understood from the very beginning that any substantive effort would entail enormous economic costs and substantial finance and technology commitments. Although China's relatively late industrialization process made it bear less responsibility than the developed world for the historical accumulation of greenhouse gases (GHGs) and ozone-depleting substances (ODS) in the atmosphere, its sheer size, as well as the high speed and magnitude of economic development since the early 1980s, had made China a major contributor and thus put the country's environmental and industrial policies under intense international scrutiny at the time of early negotiations. From 1986 to 1994, China's consumption of ODS soared from roughly 3 percent of the world total to 18 percent, while China's global ranking in terms of GHG emissions climbed from third in the late 1980s to second in the mid-1990s (Economy 1998: 270). The exorbitant economic and moral stakes relating to ozone depletion and global warming prompted the Chinese government to rethink and repackage its unsystematic policies in a way that could better serve its national interest and preserve its state image in such crucial environmental negotiations and, as a result of some inter-agency working conferences aimed at better government coordination, a cohesive set of principles and guidelines were established by the decision makers to combine developmental and international perspectives on global environmental issues. Although traditional principles like the supremacy of national sovereignty, North–South equity and the priority of developing modern industry articulated by the Foreign Ministry and the State Planning Commission (SPC) still dominated the policy-making process, a more proactive epistemic community represented by the National Environmental Protection Agency (NEPA) and State Science and Technology Commission (SSTC) was quickly emerging, focusing on climate change and ozone issues during their specialists' frequent interactions with their counterparts in the international community. Exchanges and collaborations with foreign specialist communities as well as international aid from development agencies measurably increased the Chinese understanding of global environmental challenges like climate change and the range of response measures that they considered, and in some cases actually transformed the thinking of Chinese officials (Economy 1997: 21).

As for the case of the Montreal Protocol that was put in place in 1987 and required signatory developing countries to phase out the use and production of ozone-depleting chlorofluorocarbons (CFCs) and halons by 2010, the Chinese government argued during the negotiations of the London Amendments to the Montreal Protocol in 1990 that, since developed countries were responsible for most of the ozone-depletion damage, a financial assistance mechanism should be established to financially and technically assist developing countries like China in complying with the protocol. This developmental and historical perspective accorded with the traditional principle that rich countries should offer resources and technology for implementation of environmental treaties, yet it also showed China's readiness to conditionally accept green protocols vital for the ecosystem and human health. China ratified the Vienna Convention for the Protection of the Ozone Layer in 1989, but it did not ratify the 1987 Montreal Protocol until 1991, one year after the Multilateral Fund (MLF) was established. Upon China's ratification, with the establishment of MLF as a crucial condition, the government promptly started to satisfy procedural requirements that called for China to establish institutions to organize protocol implementation, complete a country program for the phase-out of ODS, and report ODS consumption and production data to the Ozone Secretariat (Zhao 2002: 332–34). As the world's leading ODS consumer and producer at that time, China encountered enormous initial difficulties in meeting voluntary goals specified in its national program by the mid-1990s due to the fast expansion of such ODS sectors as household refrigerators, air-conditioners, and fire extinguishers. In 1996, China became the largest producer of ozone-depleting chemicals, with its overall ODS production and consumption levels exceeding targets by 94 percent and 65 percent respectively. By 1998, however, China was already below the protocol's 2002 goals for freezing halon production and consumption at average levels for the period 1995 to 1997; China also met the protocol's requirement to freeze consumption and production of CFCs beginning in July 1999 at the 1995 to 1997 average levels (Zhao 2002: 332). In the new century, China eventually met the protocol obligations successfully and froze consumption and production of CFCs and halons. On 1 July 2007, China shut down five of its six remaining ODS plants, putting the country two and a half years ahead of the Montreal Protocol's 2010 deadline for phase-out of the two ozone-depleting chemicals (UNEP 2007).

Like ozone depletion, climate change is another global atmospheric problem that demands joint action by sovereign states to cut anthropogenic emissions of gases, so the trajectories of international negotiations and cooperation over the two issues shared some similarities but, in large part, they are different from each other due to the distinct scientific uncertainties, complexities of achieving solutions, and mitigation costs. One striking distinction between the two negotiations is the timing of universal participation, which emerged in the ozone issue but became intrinsic during the climate change negotiations (Hoffmann 2005: 11). Most of the ozone talks prior to the Montreal Protocol were between the European countries and the United States due to the insignificant role of most Southern states in the production of ODS. China and many other developing countries had not become active participants until the Montreal Conference and the post-Montreal sessions, and immediately after universal participation rose to prominence, development issues began to dominate the ozone agenda (Hoffmann 2005: 11). Unlike the ozone talks that pulled in developing nations after the landmark protocol took effect, the climate change problem required universal participation in the initial stage of its international negotiations. In contrast to the early ozone negotiations that involved the participation of fewer than 40 states, most of which were northern states, the climate change negotiating process from the outset drew the attendance of more than 100 sovereign states. The participation of the global South from the start meant that development was an early and crucial aspect of the negotiations, whereas in the ozone negotiations development concerns arose much later (Hoffmann 2005: 13).

As the largest developing country in the world, China's position in the early stage of global climate negotiations had been shaped in the context of universal participation which, according to the Logic of Collective Action (Olson 1965), often entails an increasing difficulty in coordinating collective actions due to the large number of actors. Unlike ozone depletion, the climate change issue faces far more scientific uncertainties, much higher mitigation costs and may have an adverse impact on almost every economy in the world and hit severely those sectors intimately involved with fossil fuel usage, as well as some chemical and farm industries. The two global atmospheric negotiations took significantly different paths and thus produced incommensurable outcomes with distinct effects and implications. Due to the high stakes involved and the universal participation mode of international climate politics, China's climate diplomacy started in a similar mode as its ozone policy but gradually followed a divergent trajectory when the climate talks themselves entered uncharted waters.

Early stage of China's climate diplomacy

Climate change, mostly caused by increased GHG emissions from human activities since the Industrial Revolution and especially in the last half century, did not become an urgent item on the world scientific agenda until the 1970s. On 12–23 February 1979, the First World Climate Conference sponsored by the World Meteorological Organization (WMO) was held in Geneva to promote scientific understanding and public awareness of the climate change problem. The conference, mostly attended by scientists from a wide range of disciplines, triggered the establishment of the Intergovernmental Panel on Climate Change (IPCC), a scientific intergovernmental body tasked with evaluating the risk of climate change and exploring possible policy responses, by the WMO and the United Nations Environment Programme (UNEP) in 1988. Shortly after the IPCC published its first assessment report in 1990, which later served as the documentary basis of the United Nations Framework Convention on Climate Change (UNFCCC), the UN established the Intergovernmental Negotiating Committee (INC) in preparation for a framework convention on climate change. Like many other developing countries, China took part in the international climate negotiations from their preliminary stages, viewing climate change as the same type of issue as ozone depletion, involving North–South equity problems. Similarly, China believed that developed countries historically should take responsibility for climate change and therefore should provide financial and technological aid to developing countries to facilitate mitigation and adaptation. The UN-tracked climate talks, in sharp contrast to the initial ozone negotiations exclusively between rich states, were influenced by such development and history concerns due to universal participation from the outset .

As the only permanent member on the UN Security Council representing the Third World, China had been playing a leading role among developing countries in steering international climate change negotiations, uniting with other developing countries to form the "bloc of G-77 (the group of 77 developing countries) plus China," which comprises about 90 percent of the developing countries within the UNFCCC. When the INC meetings in preparation for the UNFCCC began, the Chinese delegation argued for equity on historical grounds, placing the blame primarily on the North (Dasgupta 1994: 133). From June 1991, as an aggressive opponent of a binding convention on climate change, China aligned itself closely with India in an effort to push for a convention arguing that the South bore far less responsibility than the North, whose high per capita emissions and opulent lifestyles were the primary causes of climate change. Throughout the negotiation process, the Chinese delegates remained committed to only a general framework convention that did not include the delineation of specific responsibilities or commitments for the signatories, especially with regard to curtailing emissions of the principal greenhouse gas, carbon dioxide (Economy 1997: 20). The Chinese delegation strongly opposed legally binding emission-reduction targets for developing countries in particular, and insisted that industrialized countries should provide technology and fund aid to developing countries. It advocated the preservation of national sovereignty, claiming that developing countries have the right to develop and should neither be obliged to undertake measures that might impede development nor be subject to conditions being placed on aid or development financing.

China's early diplomatic stand on climate change was in line with some established principles which had emerged as a result of the domestic debates over the country's proper strategy towards ozone depletion and other urgent ecological challenges faced by the international community. Those principles that closely resembled the traditional perspective and later on had far-reaching impact upon China's environmental diplomacy were formally established as guidelines for environmental protection for international negotiations at an inter-agency conference in Spring 1990 between the Ministry of Foreign Affairs, the NEPA, the SPC and the SSTC:

1 Environment and development should be integrated, but environmental protection should not be achieved at the expense of the economy.
2 From a historical perspective, the developed countries are responsible for global environmental degradation and the current problems with greenhouse gas emissions.

3 Developed countries should provide resources for implementation of agreements or declarations signed.
4 In order to accommodate national intellectual property rights, the governments of the developed countries should buy technology from companies and sell it to developing nations at below-market prices.
5 The sovereignty of natural resources rights must be respected and no country can interfere with the decisions of another with regard to the use of its natural resources.

(Economy 1998: 271–72)

As early as the 1992 Rio Earth Summit, China and India, speaking on behalf of other developing countries, insisted that developed countries should commit themselves to technology transfer as a condition of developing countries' support for the proposed agreements on global warming. These stances were consistent with those of other developing countries and were embodied in the UNFCCC. China's adherence to the principle of "common but differentiated responsibilities" won support and praise from developing countries, asserting its legitimacy and gaining soft power. By consolidating a coalition around itself, China could ensure that its interests would be better supported, and that it would gain international prestige as a proactive actor in environmental protection (Kobayashi 2003: 88).

Meanwhile, China also adjusted its stand when negotiating with developed countries, showing its respect for international norms of environmental protection and trying to reduce Western countries' hostility in the aftermath of the Tiananmen incident in 1989. China felt diplomatically isolated in the early 1990s. The climate change issue came into focus at the same time, thereby serving as an ideal tool for China to regain its international position (Kobayashi 2003: 91). The UNFCCC negotiations were high-profile talks, putting China in the spotlight whenever it took the initiative (Kobayashi 2003: 91). China was not only one of the first countries to formulate a domestic "Agenda 21" in 1994, mirroring the UNCED (UN Conference on Environment and Development) program on sustainable development, but it also passed the Air Pollution Law in 1996, accounting for provisions in the UNFCCC (Kobayashi 2003: 91). China thought it would gain international prestige in being proactive in environmental protection cooperation. Though refusing to accept any commitment at first, China and other developing countries agreed finally in the UNFCCC to establish national emissions inventories, report on national programs and promote cooperation, sustainable development and information exchange (United Nations 1992: 5–6). Due to long-standing suspicion that Western countries may shift their own responsibilities and use environmental issues to hamper China's economic rise, China initially opposed a new protocol on the grounds of scientific uncertainty, or the "joint implementation" programs, fearing that giving credit for reduced emissions might lessen developed countries' commitment to emissions abatement. With the ongoing international talks, China gradually changed its tough stance on these issues during the subsequent Conferences of Parties (COPs) to the UNFCCC, paving way for the 1997 Kyoto Protocol.

China's diplomatic scores from the Kyoto Protocol

After years of heated debates, delegates from 149 countries and regions passed the Kyoto Protocol in Japan in December 1997. The Kyoto Protocol is the first international treaty to set detailed legally binding obligations for industrialized nations to reduce their greenhouse gases. China completed its domestic ratification process in 2002, and appealed to other hesitant parties to ratify the protocol as soon as possible. The Kyoto Protocol came into effect in 2005, requiring 38 industrialized countries to reduce their greenhouse gas emissions between 2008 and 2012 by an average of 5.2 percent below 1990 levels. In practice, the seminal Kyoto Protocol not only helped China to gain diplomatic credit, but also offered economic reward under the Clean Development Mechanism (CDM) and incentivized the country to improve its environmental governance domestically.

The principle of "common but differentiated responsibilities" advocated by China, India and other developing countries was followed by the Kyoto Protocol, which stipulated that the CDM should encourage developed countries to provide financial and technical assistance to developing countries. Conversely, developing countries have no concrete abatement commitments. They only need to establish national emissions inventories, report on national programs and promote cooperation, sustainable development, and information exchange.

From the outcome of the international climate talks by 1997, it is easy to determine that most guidelines stipulated by the "bloc of G-77 plus China" have been included in the Kyoto Protocol, which imposed compulsory emission-cutting obligations only on developed countries. As the leading negotiator of the bloc, China's persistence and tactics throughout the tough talks won admiration and support from the Third World. The Kyoto Protocol is a triumph of China's foreign policy, showing that the country was able to use diplomatic power to formulate international rules serving its own interest (Chen 2008: 150). China certainly does not have enough hard power to coerce other developing countries into supporting its stance or to force developed countries to compromise on the climate issue. Its negotiators had to understand the basic positions of different camps and grasp the balance between compromise and perseverance to achieve the common goal of developing countries.

In contrast to the United States' withdrawal from the Kyoto Protocol, China's active participation in international cooperation on global warming has won applause from European and some other industrialized countries. China's support for global cooperation to curb global warming has special significance for the international community because of its large GHG emissions and fast-growing energy consumption. China's active participation in climate change cooperation is closely related to its concern to preserve a favorable international image as a "responsible major power." Enhancing China's international image and elevating its international stature are important goals of Chinese foreign policy. China traditionally considers solidarity with developing countries as fundamentally important, and the climate change issue has provided an unprecedented opportunity for China to boost its prestige and shore up support from developing countries as well as to enhance its relationship with developed countries (Zhang 2003: 78). China's gradual change from suspicion to support of the climate change treaty helped to improve its relations with European countries in the early 1990s, when the Tiananmen incident still had a marked impact upon such ties.

China's ratification of the Kyoto Protocol shows that it is willing to accept international norms of environmental protection, which have been gradually developed in the international community since the 1950s. China's support for the Kyoto Protocol, one of the most important international institutions in the environmental area, increased its soft power in the international arena.

Without new international institutions that provide incentives and disincentives for individual states, sovereign states tend to adopt a free-ride strategy and refuse to participate in joint efforts to combat global warming when the cost of cutting domestic emission is too high. International institutions such as the Kyoto Protocol, therefore, become essential for pulling individual states into collective actions for global welfare and overcoming the free-ride preference. Refusing to join international cooperation and institutions ranged against such negative externalities will be regarded by other states as selfish and irresponsible. The country's reputation and charisma in the international community will definitely be weakened if it is seen to be refusing to shoulder its due responsibility on global public issues.

Voluntary participation in major international institutions and compliance with established rules in the international community are essential for soft power maintenance. International institutions are "the rules that govern elements of world politics and the organizations that help implement those rules" (Keohane 1998: 82). Although the international society is still described as anarchical, with world politics being driven by the traditional exercise of state power, international institutions are increasingly important and no longer marginal. In reality, even the most powerful states are relying increasingly on international institutions – not so much on the UN as on other organizations and regimes that set rules and standards to govern specific sets of activities (Keohane 1998: 84). Institutions create the capacity for states to cooperate in mutually beneficial ways by reducing the costs of making and enforcing agreements – what economists refer to as "transaction costs" (Keohane 1998: 86). Therefore, a state's stances over various kinds of international institutions are extremely important for its soft power expansion, because this directly affects its moral stature in the eyes of other states that value cooperation in the frameworks of these institutions. The soft power of a country rests primarily on three resources: its culture, its political values, and its foreign policies (Nye 2004: 11). Whether or not to join an international institution is not only part of a country's foreign policies, it is also an indicator of its political values. The US case is a good example, showing how an international image can be badly impaired by refusing to participate in international climate institutions. In 2001, US President George W. Bush announced that his country would withdraw from the Kyoto Protocol because the deal did not include meaningful participation by key developing countries. The United States' decision to walk away unilaterally from the protocol immediately aroused enduring global anger and criticism.

After the Kyoto Protocol took effect in 2005, China had more frequent exchanges on climate change with international organizations such as the World Bank and the United Nations Development Program (UNDP), as well as the governments of Italy, Canada, France, Japan, and Germany, which helped central and local Chinese government to establish emission-reduction service centers for capacity building. The Chinese government has been conducting more training activities for officials, senior managers, and consultants to familiarize them with the procedures of environmentally friendly projects and to utilize this opportunity to absorb foreign funds and technology.

China's performances in post-Kyoto talks

When the Kyoto Protocol finally came into effect in 2005 after twists and turns, the international community had already started to consider a new climate pact to replace it after 2012 when the protocol was scheduled to expire. The tenth anniversary of the birth of the Kyoto Protocol – 2007 – was a watershed for the post-Kyoto climate change debate, as new reports then released by a UN panel established the connection between climate change and human activity with a high degree of certainty. In May 2007, more than 400 scientists and experts from about 120 countries attended a major conference held in Bangkok by the IPCC, the United Nations' leading body on climate change. Delegates finalized the third IPCC Working Group report, laying out an arsenal of anti-warming measures that had to be rushed into place to avert a disastrous spike in global temperatures. China was one of the nations under most scrutiny at the Bangkok meeting. At that meeting, China was seen by some participants as the "biggest obstacle" to approving the new report that outlined a specific strategy to charge polluters for their emissions. The report suggested that stabilizing greenhouse gas levels in the atmosphere may require polluters to be charged up to US$100 per ton of CO_2 equivalent by 2030 (IPCC 2007: 9). China had long been fending off an international accord that would impose indiscriminate carbon taxes on economic activities in all countries and thus force the country to cut emissions and scale back its economy. Beijing's fears of being targeted on climate change were heightened by the statement in April 2007 by an official of the International Energy Agency (IEA) that China could become the world's largest emitter of greenhouse gases as early as 2007 (McGregor 2007). Feeling cornered in the post-Kyoto climate politics, China responded clumsily to international censure by claiming that the European Union's target of keeping global warming within a limit of 2° C "lacks a scientific basis" (Spencer 2007).

Meanwhile, in the context of growing climate awareness, China was trying to soften its stand and improve its image through releasing its first national program on climate change in June 2007. One step forward from its previous skepticism about the certainty of global warming trend, the "National Climate Change Program," which took the Chinese government two years to formulate, used much stronger language to confirm the trend and describe the serious consequences of climate change. It admitted that "annual average air temperature has increased by 0.5 to 0.8° C during the past 100 years, which was slightly larger than the average global temperature rise" (NDRC 2007: 4). By publicizing the lengthy document, China wanted the international community to know that the Chinese government was paying intensive attention to the issue, but unique national conditions such as coal-dominated energy structure and low per capita income prevented the country from accepting mandatory emissions cutting in the current stage. Despite its refusal to shoulder quantified emissions reduction, China in its national program was putting forward some voluntary targets in energy conservation and fuel switching that could be converted to assured emissions cutting. The plan reiterated the goal in China's 11th Five-Year Plan that the country would achieve the target of 20 percent reduction of energy consumption per unit GDP by 2010. This single national target could reduce China's emissions by about 1.5 billion tons of CO_2 equivalent by 2010 (Lewis 2007: 167). The release of the national program came at a time calculated to fend off international pressures. On the same day that the program was made public, the Ministry of Foreign Affairs announced that President Hu Jintao was expected to discuss China's views and policies on global climate change during his meeting with the G-8 leaders in Germany. Meanwhile, China established a high-level leading group on climate change and energy saving in 2007 headed by Premier Wen Jiabao himself, with then Vice Premier Zeng Peiyan and State Councilor Tang Jiaxuan as his assistants. China's Foreign Ministry later announced that it had also established a leading group in charge of international work on climate change, headed by Foreign Minister Yang Jiechi. The Chinese government wanted to use these high-profile measures to show the world its intensive attention to the climate issue and mobilize its cadres which for a long time had ignored the problem. Since the UN climate change summit in Bali in December 2007 formally kicked off a new round of international negotiations to work out a new accord to replace the Kyoto Protocol, environmental activists have been hoping that major emitters like the United States, China, and India will all have quantitative emission quotas or even carbon taxes imposed by the new treaty. Having been caught in a dilemma in which both international reputation and economic growth are at stake, China has on many occasions articulated the country's adherence to the "common but differentiated responsibilities" and objected to any legal responsibility on quantifiable reductions. In their press conferences during the annual session of the National People's Congress (NPC) in 2007, both Chinese Premier Wen Jiabao and Foreign Minister Li Zhaoxing were asked by the European media about China's responsibility on the global warming issue. Neither of them made any commitment to shoulder legally binding obligations for emission reductions. At a news conference on 22 November 2007, less than one month before the Bali climate summit, Chinese Foreign Ministry spokesman Liu Jianchao said developing countries should not have to meet compulsory targets set by rich nations (Xinhua News 2007). During the Bali summit, Su Wei, a top climate expert for the government and member of the Chinese delegation, said it was unfair to ask developing nations to accept binding emissions cuts and other restrictions being urged by already industrialized states (AP News 2007a).

From China's perspective, the international effort against climate change is a two-edged sword, which can transfer funds and technology to China, as has already happened, but can also put shackles upon the giant if a disadvantageous pact arises from future negotiations. Chinese experts argue that if China accepts emission quotas like those imposed on industrialized nations in the Kyoto Protocol, it will finally pay much more than it currently gains from CDM projects to buy emission permits from other countries at a higher carbon price in the post-Kyoto period. The alternative carbon tax, if adopted in the next protocol, is expected to cost Chinese industry billions of dollars at a conservative estimate if China's economy and emissions continue to grow at the current rates. China's negotiation tactic is clear, using voluntary carbon-intensity-based targets, which are founded on the reduction of energy consumption or emissions per unit of economic output, to replace mandatory emission cuttings and ease international pressures. Because such a target is inherently indexed to the economic growth of a country and meeting this target does not directly require a decrease in economic production, this type of target is more palatable to developing countries (Lewis 2007: 166). The main limitation of an intensity-based target is that, although it can lower an emission growth trajectory below the projected business-as-usual (BAU) level, it is unlikely to result in an absolute decrease in emissions (Lewis 2007: 166).

More than 100 developing countries have been acting in concert since the early days of the global climate negotiations in order to magnify their voices and fend off pressure from industrialized nations. Although huge political, economic, and geographic disparity always existed among the Third World, they still formed the "G-77 plus China" bloc to build common positions and safeguard collective interest when negotiating with affluent Western countries. Despite its large size and special status in the UN Security Council, China has preferred to ally itself with the G-77 to deal with the complicated and new topic of climate change that was first proposed by the industrialized world. In the post-Kyoto negotiation that was officially started by the Bali summit, China will still choose to enhance such strategic solidarity with the Third World rather than deviating from the bloc and acting alone. In fact, China's alliance with the G-77 has not waned, and its willingness to step out of the pack has declined even further as its fear of being singled out grows due to increasing economic growth and energy use (Lewis 2007: 166).

As the UN-track (or Kyoto-track) climate regime is featured with quantifiable emission-cutting targets, China is planning to join more regional mechanisms on climate change that emphasize non-compulsory energy-efficiency programs. Explicitly, China still claims that global climate talks should be conducted within the framework of the United Nations but, in practice, China has become more active than before in joining all kinds of bilateral and multilateral cooperation mechanisms against climate change outside the UN-track.

Multilaterally, China is more willing to accept international agreements that call for voluntary actions rather than those with mandatory emissions-cutting targets.

These will help China to enhance soft power while not harming its hard power (economic growth). In 2005, China joined collective action with Australia, India, Japan, South Korea, and the United States to establish the Asia-Pacific Partnership on Clean Development and Climate, which emphasized energy conservation and technology cooperation instead of setting mandatory emissions-cutting targets. The United States and Australia, two of its members, refused to ratify the Kyoto Protocol at that time. The Asia-Pacific Partnership on Clean Development and Climate is a cooperation mechanism outside the UNFCCC and Kyoto Protocol, and by joining this organization, China obtains advanced energy-efficiency technology from affluent countries, coordinates diplomatic positions with other heavyweights in international climate talks and improves its international image in the green area without accepting legally binding targets. In recent years, many existing multilateral organizations including APEC (Asia-Pacific Economic Cooperation), ASEAN (Association of Southeast Asian Nations) Plus Three (China, Republic of Korea, and Japan), and G-8 started to build up special mechanisms on climate change, and China has proved to be an active participant or dialogist in forums, conferences, and cooperation programs held by these mechanisms. In the APEC summit in Sydney in September 2007, both China and the United States accepted a program with non-binding goals on energy efficiency and afforestation.

In the bilateral context, China pays more attention to cooperative programs on clean energy and emission reduction with industrialized nations including the United States. The climate change issue has become an indispensable subject of China's recent bilateral talks with many Western countries. China also enhances bilateral coordination and cooperation with India and other developing powers on the climate issue. During Indian Prime Minister Manmohan Singh's visit to China in January 2008, climate change was also on the agenda and the two sides reached consensus that neither China nor India should be obligated to make commitments to reduce carbon emissions.

China is definitely facing greater challengers and pressures than before in the ongoing international climate talks. China's economic strength has grown so rapidly in the past decade that the international community expect it to shoulder correspondingly greater international responsibilities in the area of climate change. Although there seems to be a long way to go before China can accept legally binding targets for emission reductions, state leaders understand very clearly that its soft power will be greatly damaged if it continues unchanged. China is trying to gain more support and sympathy from both developed and developing countries through frequent diplomatic exchanges and to make real ongoing domestic efforts to cut carbon emissions per GDP unit in the hope of reaching zero carbon growth by the middle of this century.

Carbon intensity goal and implications

Although China's climate change policy is particularly driven by self-interest and self-defensive, seemingly leaving little room for significant compromises or changes, the country, in response to rising international pressures and domestic energy security issues, has shown a certain flexibility and shrewdness in coping with the newly emerged challenges. To improve its image in global climate politics before the Copenhagen Climate Summit, China, for the first time, declared that it was targeting a hefty 40–45 percent cut in carbon intensity, the amount of CO_2 emitted per dollar of GDP, by 2020 as compared with a 2005 baseline. Such a carbon-intensity pledge, having been met with praise and criticism internationally, is inherently indexed to the economic growth of a country and meeting this target does not directly require a decrease in economic production. The main limitation of an intensity-based target is that, although it can lower an emission growth trajectory below the projected business-as-usual level, it is unlikely to result in an absolute decrease in emissions. A carbon-intensity target is especially attractive to many developing countries that seek a transition to a low-carbon economy without taking on quantifiable emission-reduction commitments.

China's carbon-intensity target, described by Greenpeace as "not enough" (Greenpeace 2009), could be significant given the post-Kyoto context that neither the Bali Action Plan nor the Copenhagen Accord requires developing countries to formulate overarching goals for the economy. Changes in carbon intensity can arise from technological changes and through structural changes in the economy, such as a move from heavy industry to services. China has already included the goal of cutting carbon intensity by 17 percent by 2015 as a binding target in its 12th Five-Year Plan, which was passed by the National People's Congress, the top legislature, in 2011. This has made its legal position equivalent to many industrialized nations' Kyoto commitments that have been transformed into domestic legislation. It is true that, as China's GDP continues to grow rapidly, its total carbon emissions will also grow over the next decade even if carbon intensity has dropped significantly from the 2005 baseline, and the faster the economic growth is, the more carbon dioxide the country will emit. However, considering China's low per capita emissions and its exemption from legally binding targets, such a pledge is a strong one that could bring about considerable emission reduction from the BAU line calculated before additional mitigation measures are put in place. The target, if strictly enforced, will help the largest carbon emitter to avert the "no effort" scenario, and is therefore in line with the call from the Intergovernmental Panel on Climate Change for the substantial reduction of developing country emissions below BAU.

The real impact of this carbon-intensity goal on China's absolute emissions will largely depend on the exact 2005 baseline figures yet to be released by the government as well as the actual annual GDP growth rate to be fulfilled over the next decade. For example, if the annual growth rate were 6 percent, total emissions could be 30–40 percent higher and still meet the carbon intensity target, whereas at 8 percent per year they could increase by 75–90 percent over the 15-year period from the base year, and still meet the intensity target (Seligsohn and Levin 2010: 3). Another uncertainty exists in respect of the exact official 2005 baseline figure, which is yet to be published by the Chinese government. Although China has refuted emission data from the International Energy Agency and other foreign organizations, it is still in the process of conducting its own greenhouse gas emissions inventory, which will be submitted as part of its Second Communication to the UNFCCC. China may need to establish the 2005 baseline calculation before a full 2005 inventory is complete, and this next inventory should give the Chinese government a more precise figure on which to base its target (Seligsohn and Levin 2010: 2). China was using 2005 as its base year partly because, from 2001 to 2005, its energy intensity, an indicator positively correlated to variations in carbon intensity, had been steadily on the rise due to the shift of its economic structure to heavy and chemical industry. China's energy intensity started to drop again after 2006 thanks to a number of cooling-down policies and the development of green industry. The decision to use the peak figure in 2005 as the baseline may make the goal easier to fulfill. Many analysts have agreed that a higher GDP growth rate would make the target easier to reach, simply because growth adds new, more efficient and less carbon-intensive infrastructure, and the higher the growth rate, the larger the share of new and energy-efficient capital equipment in the economy as a whole (Chandler and Wang 2009: 3; Seligsohn and Levin 2010: 5).

Bringing down carbon intensity and improving energy efficiency are actually the main elements of China's long-pursuing "no regret" strategy, which implies actions providing fringe benefits to the country regardless of whether the threat of global warming is real. Climate change is not only an environmental issue for China, but also a good opportunity to address the country's serious energy shortage problem caused by growing demand, inefficient use and limited energy reserves. The relationship between economic growth and energy utilization matters greatly, not only from an emissions perspective, but also from an energy security perspective (Lewis 2007: 156). Currently the world's largest energy consumer, China is a country rich in coal but lacking in oil and natural gas. Although China is still able to supply over 90 percent of the energy it needs for industrialization and urbanization, in the long run, energy scarcity could become a real bottleneck for China's sustainable development due to its increasing dependency on imported oil and even coal, and lower-than-average per capita energy resources. China's per capita average of both coal and hydropower resources is 50 percent of the world's average, while the per capita average of both oil and natural gas resources is only one-fifteenth of the world's average (Penn 2007). About half of China's oil consumption is imported, and it has become a major coal and natural gas importer. China's primary energy demand is projected to more than double from 1,742 Mtoe in 2005 to 3,819 Mtoe in 2030 – an average annual growth rate of 3.2 percent (IEA 2007: 6).

Energy policies have dominated China's development strategy for a long time and today the government exploits global concern about climate change as a golden opportunity to improve energy efficiency and boost clean energy production. When such "no regret" policies were designed, policy makers might have placed emphasis on economic factors such as energy supply and jobs rather than the environment, but in practice, these "no-regret" options, assisted through CDM projects and subsequently the new energy strategy, may be functioning as an efficient means of slowing down the country's greenhouse gas growth and gaining competitive positions in the clean energy sector.

2 Is China's negotiating position responsible?

Since the beginning of its participation in the UN-track climate negotiations in the early 1990s, China, despite its own fast-changing economic and energy scenario and the vicissitudes in the international political arena after the end of the Cold War, has been consistent in its position that, as a developing country, it will not make any legally binding commitments to reduce its greenhouse gas emissions. China's official stance has not changed much in all previous Conferences of Parties (COPs) to the United Nations Framework Convention on Climate Change (UNFCCC), with its insistence on the Principle of Common but Differentiated Responsibilities as its non-negotiable guideline that includes the following core elements (NDRC 2009a; Hatch 2003: 50):

1. Developed countries shall take responsibility for their historical cumulative emissions and current high per capita emissions and, therefore, shall undertake legally binding quantified emission reduction commitments and provide financial support and transfer technology to developing countries.
2. Developing countries, including China, in pursuing economic development and poverty eradication, shall be exempted from legally binding obligations when taking proactive measures to adapt to and mitigate climate change.
3. The fulfillment of commitments by developed countries to provide financing, technology transfer, and capacity building support to developing countries is a condition *sine qua non* for developing countries to effectively mitigate, and adapt to, climate change.

Now the problem is whether China's insistence on exemption from compulsory emission reductions is still a fair and responsible negotiating stance when the rising power is emitting much more carbon than previously into the atmosphere and scientists are depicting a gloomier picture of global climate change.

Image change: from Kyoto Protocol signatory to largest carbon emitter

China has ratified the UNFCCC and the Kyoto Protocol, the two keystone climate accords that supported the Principle of Common but Differentiated Responsibilities and treated China as a developing country that has no compulsory emissions-cutting obligations under either accord. Although China's climate position in the past two decades has never deviated from the rest of the developing world, mainstream international opinion, once quite positive towards China's climate change strategy, has turned around dramatically and adversely since the country's speedy economic growth – mostly driven by heavy industries since the beginning of this century – has made China the largest emitter of greenhouse gases in the world, a position that had been long occupied by the United States, the world's largest economy. Since the day it joined international climate change negotiations, China has held a very skeptical view of climate change issues, with stress on the major scientific uncertainties that still surround the climate change debate. Some domestic experts even argued that global warming might bring benefits to China, because the prevailing westerly summer wind coming off the ocean will bring higher rainfall, thus benefiting areas where drought is a problem (Zhou 1997: 18–19). At the first Intergovernmental Negotiating Committee (INC) meeting in February 1991, Chinese representatives made clear their opposition to any initiative that would establish emissions ceilings for countries, regardless of whether they were developed or developing (Hatch 2003: 51). Yet such positions in the initial stage of climate talks were not immutable and China soon modified its position and accepted that only industrialized nations would be bound by emissions targets. Though refusing initially to accept any commitments, China finally agreed to the UNFCCC: to establish national emissions inventories, report on national programs, promote cooperation, and form sustainable development and information exchange (United Nations 1992: 5–6). At the start of the UN-track climate negotiations, working on the first legal document to set compulsory emissions reduction obligations, China once opposed a new protocol on the grounds of scientific uncertainty, or the joint implementation programs. Shadowed by the long-term suspicion that Western countries might shirk their own responsibilities and use environmental issues to hamper its economic rise, China feared that giving credit for reduced emissions might lessen developed countries' commitment to emissions abatement. Largely owing to the Chinese government's eagerness to rebuild its national image as a responsible major power after the 1989 Tiananmen incident, the country gradually modified its tough stance on these issues in the following Conferences of Parties (COPs) to the UNFCCC, paving the way for the consensus on the Kyoto Protocol in 1997.

China's willingness to temper its original hard-line positions on compromises and support of the two most important climate treaties has gained diplomatic credit in the international community. As the lead negotiator of the "bloc of G-77 plus China," China's persistence and tactics throughout the tough talks have won admiration and support from the Third World, because most of the guidelines insisted on by the developing countries have been incorporated into the UNFCCC and the Kyoto Protocol. The climate change issue has provided an unprecedented opportunity for China to boost its prestige and shore up support from developing countries as well as enhance its relationship with developed countries (Zhang 2003: 78). In contrast to the United States' withdrawal from the Kyoto Protocol, China's active participation in international cooperation on global warming has won applause from European and other industrialized countries. China's gradual change from suspicion to support of the climate change treaty helped to improve its relations with European countries in the 1990s, given the ever-present residual hostilities affecting such ties stemming from the Tiananmen incident. China's support for global cooperation to curb global warming has special meaning to the international community because of its large GHG emissions and fast-growing energy consumption.

Nevertheless, China's favorable international image in the early stage of international climate negotiations has been changed dramatically and adversely since the country's total energy consumption and carbon emissions started to grow very rapidly after China's accession to the World Trade Organization (WTO) at the end of 2001. Although China had made remarkable achievements in constantly bringing down its energy intensity (ratio of energy consumption to GDP) from 1980 to 2000, such a trend reversed between 2002 to 2005, and energy growth surpassed economic growth for the first time in decades (Lewis 2007: 156). In 2007 as the Fourth Assessment Report (AR4) released by the IPCC stated that the global warming process since the mid-twentieth century is unequivocal and is very likely due to the observed increase in anthropogenic greenhouse gas concentrations, China meanwhile was firmly entrenched as one of earth's most flagrant offenders since its fossil-fuel CO_2 emissions had grown a remarkable 92.0 percent from 2000 to 2007, a year when China for the first time overtook the United States as the world's largest carbon emitter (US Carbon Dioxide Information Analysis Center 2011b). During a major IPCC climate conference held in Bangkok in May 2007 to finalize its working group report, China was seen by some of the 400 participating scientists and experts from about 120 countries as a major obstacle to approving the new report that outlined a specific strategy to charge polluters for their emissions. The report suggested that stabilizing greenhouse gas levels in the atmosphere would require polluters to be charged up to US$100 per ton of CO_2 equivalent by 2030. Some participants greeted with deep dismay China's seemingly pessimistic and obstructionist approach at the event (AFP News 2007). Since then, China has been under greater scrutiny in almost every international climate convention because of its uncompromising refusal to cap its carbon emissions coupled with its fast-growing share in global total emissions. Although China unveiled its first firm target for reducing its carbon intensity by 40–45 percent by the year 2020 based on 2005 levels two weeks before the Copenhagen Climate Summit in 2009, China was blamed by many international media for wrecking the last-ditch talks and lacking sincerity in its intentions of working out a binding treaty on emission cuttings (*Guardian* 2009; *Telegraph* 2009; *Spiegel Online International* 2010). China has on many occasions found itself labeled as the villain. The Chinese Premier Wen Jiabao's diplomatic snub of absenting himself from the decisive closed-door meeting of world leaders in Copenhagen's Bella Center and instead only sending a second-tier official in the country's foreign ministry to sit opposite US President Obama, was interpreted as an obvious affront to heads of states from two dozen countries that were serious about negotiating ways to protect the world's climate. During the session, which dragged on for ten hours, the world's most powerful heads of state were forced to wait around as the Chinese delegate left the meeting to make telephone calls to his superiors (*Guardian* 2009).

In sharp contrast to its previous flexible and accommodating stances in the early stage of the international climate negotiations, China's blunt performances and increasing assertiveness in the post-Kyoto talks reflect its awareness of being addicted to dazzling economic growth driven by energy-intensive and highly polluting industries as well as the concomitant anxiety about being besieged by other state and non-state players in the international community with growing concern over gloomy climate change projections.

Why point the finger at China?

As the world's largest carbon emitter, China contributed about 24 percent of the global total CO_2 emissions from the burning of fossil fuels and cement manufacture in 2009, seven percentage points higher than the emissions share of the United States (Figure 2.1; US Carbon Dioxide Information Analysis Center 2011a), the second largest emitter, that had been notorious for its high-carbon lifestyle for decades. Moreover, in the first decade of the twenty-first century, China had more than doubled its carbon emissions (Figure 2.2; US Carbon Dioxide Information Analysis Center 2011a); if such a trend continues, most of the mitigation effect contributed by industrialized nations through cutting their emissions compulsorily might be neutralized by the newly added greenhouse gas emissions from China alone. The logic that size and growth rate do matter in terms of global emissions control has made China one of the most important nations under scrutiny of the international community, which fears that the unchecked emissions increase of the emerging superpower might jeopardize the fair play of global actions against climate change. However, China is still using its low cumulative and per capita emissions as an excuse not to shoulder any compulsory mitigation obligations, as it often says on the basis of equity, the share of global emissions originating from developing countries (including China) should be allowed to grow to meet their social and development needs (National Development and Reform Commission 2007: 2). China's National Climate Change Programme quoted the World Resource Institute (WRI) as saying that its "cumulative emissions of CO_2 from fossil fuel combustion accounted for only 9.33 percent of the world total during the period of 1950–2002, and the cumulative CO_2 emissions per capita are 61.7 tons over the same period, ranking the 92nd in the world" (National Development and Reform Commission 2007: 6). Yet China's dazzling economic boom, driven by massive industrialization and urbanization since the beginning of the present century, has not only pushed up its energy demand and total carbon emissions, as it were, overnight, but also boosted the populous country's per capita emissions at almost the same rate (Figure 2.3; US Carbon Dioxide Information Analysis Center 2011a) due to the relatively stabilized total population. In 2004, China's per capita CO_2 emissions from fossil-fuel combustion were still equivalent to only 87 percent of the world average (National Development and Reform Commission 2007: 6), while two years later, in 2006, China's per capita emission rate (1.27 metric tons of carbon) for the first time exceeded the global average (1.25 metric tons of carbon), and, in 2007, China's per capita fossil-fuel emissions increased by

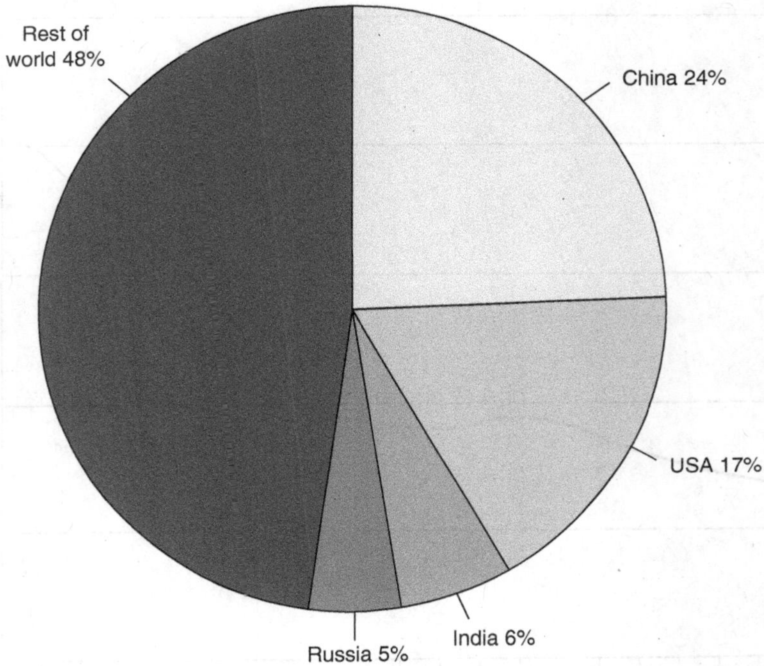

Figure 2.1 Share of top four emission countries in total global carbon emissions in 2009.

6.4 percent to 1.35 metric tons of carbon, ranked 81 in the world and more than half of that of Germany, estimated at 2.61 metric tons (US Carbon Dioxide Information Analysis Center 2011b). Should such a rate be maintained, China's per capita carbon emissions would be expected to exceed those of Germany by 2017. Therefore, the international community that imposes intense pressures upon China in global climate bargaining not only worries about the immense size of China's total emissions but, more importantly, is deeply concerned about the country's rapid growth in carbon emissions.

Another factor that has led to finger-pointing at China is the country's economic and technological inefficiency, indicated by its exorbitant energy and emissions intensity, which refers to the amount of energy consumption and CO_2 emissions needed for every unit of Gross Domestic Product (GDP). Although China had made constant progress in reducing its energy and carbon intensity until 2001, its energy and carbon intensity actually went up in the next few years because the huge spike in overseas demand for Chinese goods immediately after its entry into the World Trade Organization spurred China to shift to heavy and chemical industries – without much investment in modern technologies – in order

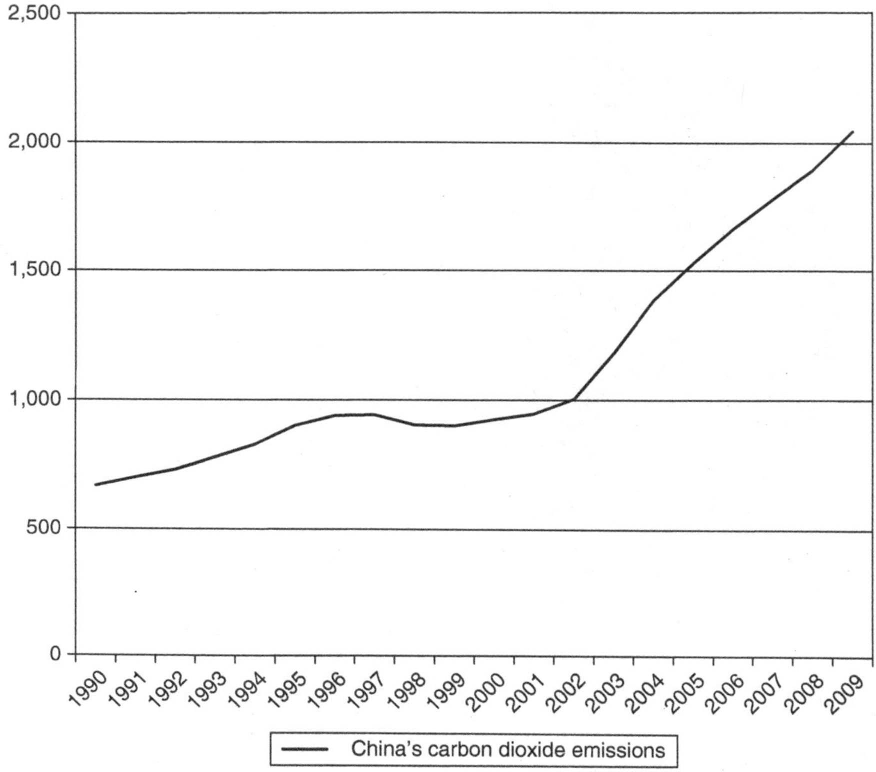

Figure 2.2 China's total CO_2 emissions since 1990 (million metric tons of carbon).

to keep prices competitively low. China's total energy consumption has been growing at a breakneck pace, jumping from half that of the United States to being the world's largest consumer in just ten years from 2001 to 2010. Besides, China's energy mix has a structural problem: about 70 percent of the country's primary energy consumption comes from coal, which is inherently more polluting and more carbon-intensive than oil and gas. According to figures from the US Energy Information Administration (EIA), in 2006, China on average emitted 2.85 metric tons of CO_2 when producing 1,000 US dollars (year 2000) of GDP, more than five times the emissions in the United States for the same unit of GDP and more than ten times that in Japan (US Energy Information Administration 2008). This figure, about 19 percent higher than China's own carbon intensity in 2001, also exceeds the average level for the African continent and the whole world by 114 percent and 270 percent respectively in the same year (US Energy Information Administration 2008). Even if China is able to reach its short-term goal of cutting carbon intensity by 40 to 45 percent between 2005 and 2020, it

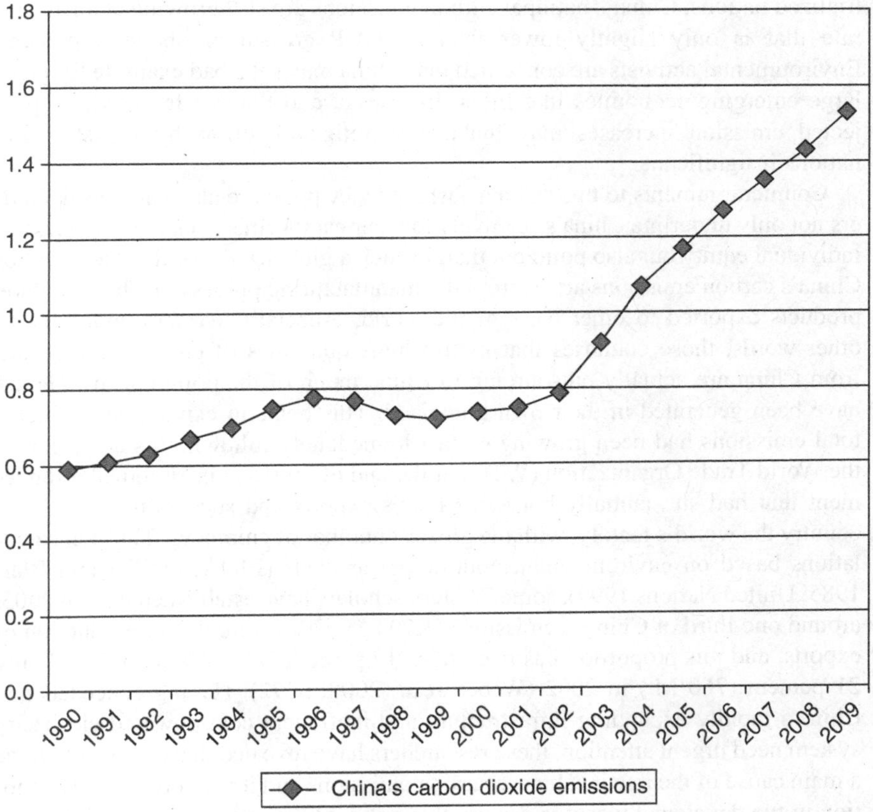

Figure 2.3 China's per capita CO_2 emissions since 1990 (metric tons of carbon).

will still generate far more carbon emissions per unit of GDP than the world's average, not to mention the emissions of the industrialized nations.

China bashing: fair or not?

International climate change politics since its beginning has been a finger-pointing game, in which China often finds itself in the eye of the storm, either being blamed for irresponsibility or leading accusations that rich nations are trying to sabotage climate talks. The grim fact that China has surpassed the United States and become the world's largest carbon emitter seems to have had a substantial impact on the global public's psychology in an era which demonstrates growing climate consciousness. The traditional bloc of developing nations is no longer monolithic, with more and more members seeing China as among the developed countries in terms of its responsibility to reduce carbon emissions. In sharp contrast to the flattened or even decreasing trend of total emissions in most industrialized nations, China's national carbon emissions are still growing at an annual rate that is only slightly lower than its GDP growth of above 8 percent. Environmental activists are concerned that China may set a bad example for other large emerging economies like India, Indonesia, and South Africa, whose projected emission increases may make any mitigation effort by industrialized nations insignificant.

Counterarguments to this "China bashing" viewpoint are also valid, as defenders not only underline China's relatively low per capita emissions in the context of individual equity but also point out that, in such a globalized world, a large part of China's carbon emissions arises from the manufacturing process of Chinese-made products exported to other parts of the world, especially Western countries. In other words, those countries that import huge quantities of cheap commodities from China are actually outsourcing to China much of the pollution that should have been generated in their own homeland. This helps to explain why China's total emissions had been growing so fast immediately following its accession to the World Trade Organization (WTO) at the end of 2001, an institutional arrangement that had substantially boosted China's exports and successfully made the country the world's factory, with the greatest number of chimneys. Through calculations based on environmental input-output analysis (EIOA) (Miller and Blair 1985; United Nations 1999), some Western scholars have established that, in 2005, around one-third of Chinese emissions (1,700 Mt CO_2) were due to production of exports, and this proportion has risen from 12 percent (230 Mt) in 1987 and only 21 percent (760 Mt) in 2002 (Weber *et al.* 2008: 3572). Having conceded that China's rapidly expanding infrastructure and inefficient coal-powered electricity system need urgent attention, these researchers have revealed that exports could be a main cause of the rise in Chinese carbon emissions and it is likely that consumption in the developed world is driving this trend. Other studies on this topic have reached similar conclusions. Some analysis showed that, due to China's large trade surplus and the relatively high carbon intensity, net exports accounted for 23 percent of China's total CO_2 emissions in 2004 (Watson and Wang 2007). It was a figure comparable to Japan's total CO_2 emissions, and more than double the UK's emissions in the same year (Watson and Wang 2007). The equivalent yearly emissions figures after that could be even larger, as China's trade surplus continued to soar until the global financial crisis in 2008. The analysis prepared by two scientists at the US National Center for Atmospheric Research suggested that, during 1997–2003, US carbon emissions would have increased from 3 percent to 6 percent if the goods imported from China had been produced in the United States, while about 7–14 percent of China's current carbon emissions were a result of producing exports for US consumers (Shui and Harriss 2006: 4063). Almost all of these studies suggested that a globalized economy means that a country's carbon footprint is international and countries, especially developed countries, should also be concerned with emissions beyond their borders. In fact, the transfer of advanced green technologies and expertise relating to clean energy and emission reduction from industrialized nations to developing countries would be an effective solution to the mitigation of global carbon emissions. Improved international accounting methodologies for assigning responsibility for carbon emissions must be designed to consider the dynamic nature of international trade (Shui and Harriss 2006: 4063).

Being both a major culprit and victim in climate politics, China deserves credit for supporting the Kyoto Protocol and adjusting its stand to acclimatize itself to the changing situation, but given a bleak international climate outlook and China's alarming energy and emission trajectory, Chinese planners need to keep open the possibility of making larger concessions to ensure that Chinese emissions peak and then decline within two decades. China's open pledge of a 40–45 percent cut in carbon intensity by 2020 is a half-step deviation from its decade-long insistence on the principle of "common but differentiated responsibility," which has long been used by the developing world to bargain with wealthy nations for exemption from legally binding obligations. The country may need to commit more as its dazzling economic growth is defeating the government's claim of being a developing economy and more and more Chinese citizens are catching up with the average living standards in high-income nations. Given the substantial disparity in per capita income and emissions among different provinces, China, as a vast continental state, is actually facing a mitigation dilemma very similar to that which the world is facing. Just like the northern bloc of industrialized nations, wealthy provinces located in the eastern part of China have higher per capita income, emissions and advanced technology compared with the less developed provinces in western China. The UNFCCC and Kyoto Protocol have helped the developed North and developing South to share differentiated responsibility in the fight against climate change, but there is no such institutional arrangement to ensure similar responsibility sharing and emissions trading within the sovereign state of China which is almost the same size as Europe. To be fairer, the 31-province country should no longer be treated as a monolithic state actor in future climate negotiations aimed at assigning emission rebate quotas within the international community. Otherwise the richer Chinese provinces could always use the impoverished hinterland as the best excuse to evade mitigation obligations, even when their per capita incomes are on a par with many industrialized nations.

3 China's energy and environmental bureaucracy

China's climate change policy is part of its energy and environmental strategy, which in turn is driven by the country's overall economic growth targets. Given the profound impact on a broad set of interest groups in the party-state, climate-related policies are often the outcome of bureaucratic politics and inter-agency competition within the regime rather than reasoned debate. Inside the Chinese government – overwhelmed by the strategic priority of modernizing the economy – economic and energy departments have played a predominant role in shaping the country's climate policy, while environmental administration from central to local government is subordinate in the policy process. In recent years, although environmental non-governmental organizations (ENGOs) and the emerging civil society have become increasingly visible players in China's green politics, their roles and functions are still marginal under China's state-centric political systems.

Evolution of China's inter-agency mechanism on climate change

China's one-party political system predetermines the country's policy process on many issues. In the inter-relations between the ruling Chinese Communist Party (CCP), the legislature (National People's Congress), and the cabinet (State Council), the CCP apparatus led by its Politburo, a core group of about 25 top leaders, always plays a predominant role in decision-making processes with its members penetrating the legislature and the cabinet and its ruling status stipulated by the Constitution. State Council commissions and line ministries are responsible for routine and detailed administrative work and are very powerful in terms of their influence on the final policy outcome by providing consultancy and proposing policy drafts in their issue areas, but they still have to heed the Politburo's voices during decision making on important or controversial issues. Compared with the National People's Congress (NPC), that is the least powerful branch among the three and often tabbed as "rubber stamp," the State Council that sits atop a vast bureaucracy including virtually all ministries, commissions, and other administrative agencies, and thus has considerable access to expertise and resources (Ma and Ortolano 2000: 14), plays an even more influential legislative role when drafting proposed laws and referring them to the NPC.

The State Council is made up of a number of functional units (ministries, commissions, administration, bureaus, and departments), which are in charge of various issues such as foreign affairs, economic planning, education, public health, finance, land resources, personnel, and environmental protection. When dealing with complex issues related to different administrative departments, the Chinese government usually establishes ad hoc inter-agency mechanisms for coordination and cooperation among the participants, with one or two ministerial departments playing a leading role. China, for example, has established the State Flood Control and Drought Relief Headquarters to coordinate anti-flood and drought-relief work among various ministries and departments, with the Ministry of Water Resources functioning as the pivotal department and taking charge of the daily administrative work of the Headquarters. In the case of climate change that relates to such realms as environment, energy, technology, meteorology, and foreign affairs, China has set up ad hoc inter-ministerial mechanisms since the 1980s to direct and coordinate work among the primary actors involved in shaping policy responses to the international climate agenda. China's "development-first" climate stance is closely related to the interactive structure of its inter-agency mechanism on climate change, in which the National Development and Reform Commission (NDRC), a macroeconomic and energy management agency, has been playing a pivotal role, while the Ministry of Environmental Protection, successor to the State Environmental Protection Administration (SEPA), and China Meteorological Administration (CMA), are marginalized.

In the beginning, China treated climate change as a scientific issue and made the CMA responsible for advising the government on policy options in the international arena involving the UNFCCC. As political awareness and economic sensitivity surrounding climate change increased in the late 1990s, this role was shifted to the more powerful State Development and Planning Commission, which has since evolved into the NDRC (Lewis 2007: 158). In 1998, China established the National Coordination Committee on Climate Change, an ad hoc inter-agency organization that later included representatives from the NDRC, Foreign Ministry, Ministry of Science and Technology, CMA, SEPA, and other ten ministerial-level departments (Figure 3.1).

With the NDRC director appointed as the Chairman of the National Coordination Committee on Climate Change, the NDRC had been managing all routine affairs of the Committee and clearly had the pivotal role in the decision-making process. SEPA ranked fifth in the agency pecking order within the National Coordination Committee on Climate Change, behind the NDRC, Foreign Ministry, Ministry of Science and Technology, and CMA. Compared with SEPA and CMA, which were potentially sympathetic to the more proactive approach of emission abatement, the NDRC leans toward rapid economic growth as well as materialized benefits including fund and technology transfers.

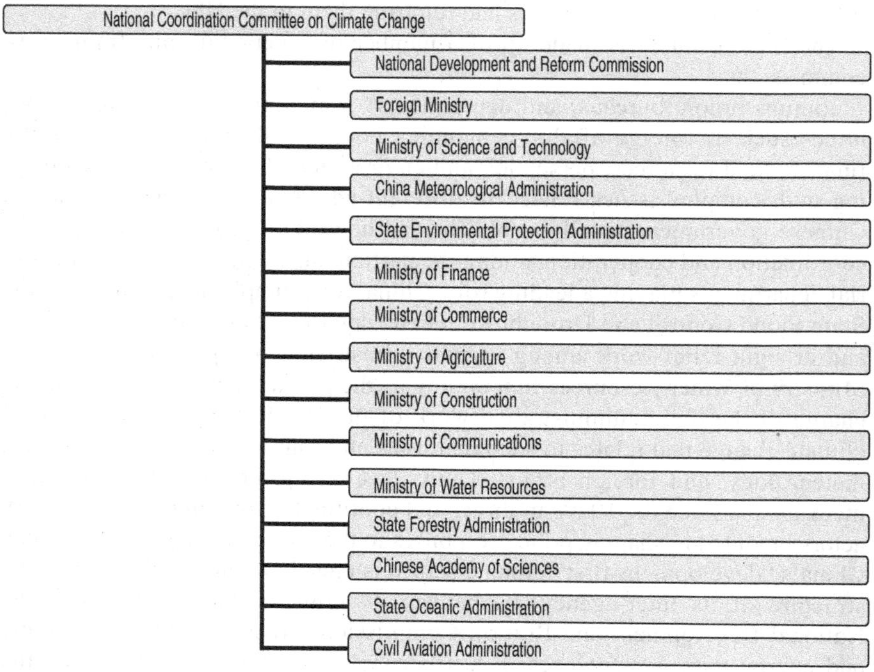

Figure 3.1 China's inter-agency mechanism on climate change before 2007.

The main function of the NDRC, a macro-economic regulatory department, is to maximize economic development driven by an expanding energy supply. From its inception, the NDRC was very skeptical toward scientific opinion on the causes and impacts of climate change, and it opposed any commitments not in line with economic growth, e.g. greenhouse gas emission reductions (Richerzhagen and Scholz 2007: 318).

Inter-agency conflicts between the NDRC and SEPA have become pronounced as domestic environmental issues increase. An evident inconsistency between the pro-energy commission and pro-environment administration was China's car fuel policy which went awry in 2007. Vigorously pushed by SEPA, the central government had planned, on July 1, 2007, to introduce a standard for cars known as Euro III, which would reduce carbon monoxide and other emissions. The NDRC, however, in 2007, proposed that the rules should be delayed for up to two years because of the lack of compatible fuel – given that the changes could damage new engines (Chen 2009a: 22).

The high-powered role of the Foreign Ministry and Ministry of Science and Technology enhances NDRC's advantageous position in the climate change decision-making process. The Foreign Ministry puts an emphasis on the preservation of national sovereignty, meaning that developing countries have the need and

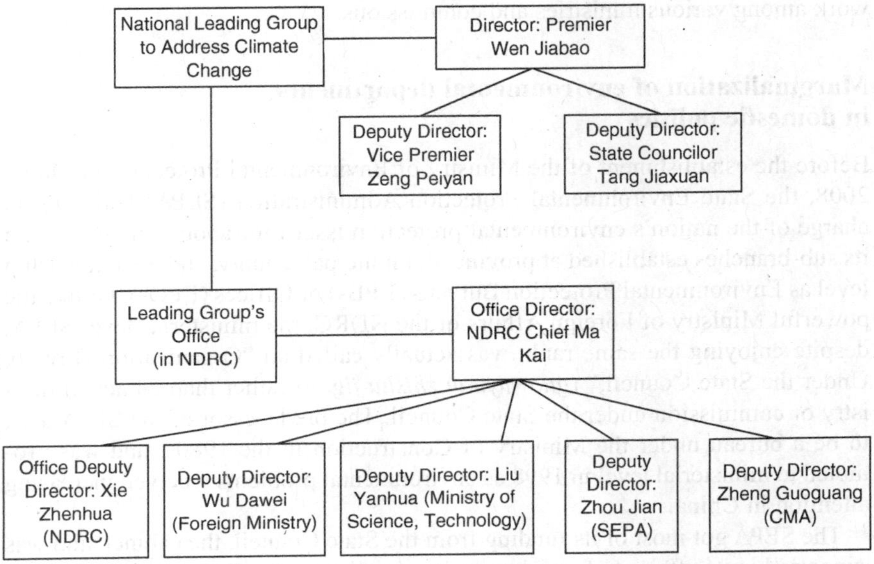

Figure 3.2 Inter-agency mechanism on climate change after June 2007.

the right to develop and China should not succumb to Western pressures for further mitigation actions; while the Ministry of Science and Technology focuses on foreign technological aid and transfer. Without any structural change to the inter-agency climate change mechanism, the "development-first" views of the NDRC and Foreign Ministry will undoubtedly continue to shape the major features of China's negotiating position in international talks.

Under pressure from the international community on account of its rapidly growing carbon emissions, China decided to upgrade the existing inter-agency climate mechanism to a higher level in 2007, when the National Leading Group on Energy Saving, Emission Cutting and Climate Change was set up and headed by Premier Wen Jiabao himself instead of a ministerial-level official from the NDRC. The National Leading Group on Energy Saving, Emission Cutting and Climate Change does put more emphasis on the environment aspect in response to the grim climate context, but the NDRC's predominant position in the policy-making process has not changed significantly, as the National Leading Group still houses its administrative office within the NDRC. The pro-growth feature concerning China's climate policy-making mechanism remains untouched due to the lack of significant structural changes inside the National Leading Group, which was headed by the Premier, whose principal task was to boost the economy and create more jobs, and his two associates, Vice Premier Zeng Peiyan with an NDRC background and State Councilor Tang Jiaxuan, promoted from the post of Foreign Minister (Figure 3.2). The NDRC Chief was still the director of the National Leading Group's administrative office in charge of coordination work among various ministries and commissions.

Marginalization of environmental departments in domestic politics

Before the establishment of the Ministry of Environmental Protection in March 2008, the State Environmental Protection Administration (SEPA) had been in charge of the nation's environmental protection issues for about ten years, with its sub-branches established at provincial, municipal, county, and even township level as Environmental Protection Bureaus (EPBs) or Offices (EPOs). Unlike the powerful Ministry of Foreign Affairs or the NDRC, the ministerial-level SEPA, despite enjoying the same rank, was actually called an "Organization Directly Under the State Council," (*guowuyuan zhishu jigou*) rather than an actual ministry or commission under the State Council. The predecessor of the SEPA used to be a bureau under the Ministry of Construction in the 1980s, and was promoted to ministerial level in 1998 as environmental problems received increasing attention in China.

The SEPA got most of its funding from the State Council, the cabinet, and was supported in its efforts to formulate national policy by the Committee on Natural Resources and Environmental Protection under China's top legislature, the National People's Congress. The SEPA had proved to be a weak unit inside the State Council, compared with other ministries or commissions in the true sense, such as the NDRC, the Ministry of Commerce, or the Ministry of Agriculture. China's "development-first" strategy predetermines the dominant role of economic departments in the inter-agency policy process, while those like the SEPA and China Meteorological Administration (CMA) play minor roles.

As SEPA was not a fully fledged ministry, its representatives usually could not join cabinet-level decision-making processes through the two normal forms of State Council conferences: the State Council Executive Conference and the State Council Plenary Conference. Every week, the State Council holds its regular executive conference to discuss current issues, with participation of the Premier, vice premiers, state councilors and the secretary-general to the State Council. The State Council Plenary Conference also includes chiefs of ministries, commissions, the central bank, and the National Audit Office inside the cabinet. Hence, the inclusion of a government department in the cabinet is crucial for its influences upon decision making at a central level.

Pollution control functions in China have been scattered among several ministerial departments including environmental protection, water resources, construction, agriculture, oceanic, and forestry. It is the Ministry of Foreign Affairs that is in charge of talks on international environmental treaties, and it is the National Development and Reform Commission (NDRC) that is responsible for the environmental industry, energy efficiency, climate change, and carbon emission cutting issues. The protection of water resources including rivers and lakes is the business of the Ministry of Water Resources, while the Bureau of Forestry takes care of ecological protection in the woods and forests. The environmental protection of oceans, rural soil and water, and urban water and refuse treatment is respectively in the hands of the Oceanic Administration, the Ministry of Agriculture, and the Ministry of Housing and Urban–Rural Development (formerly known as the Ministry of Construction). The Ministry of Finance is in charge of government fund investment in environmental protection, while the Meteorological Administration is authorized to carry out nationwide air quality supervision. Although three ministries, namely the Ministry of Water Resources, the Ministry of Housing and Urban–Rural Development, and the Ministry of Agriculture have been involved in urban and rural water management, it is the Ministry of Health that takes charge of drinking water safety issues in cities and the countryside. The SEPA, therefore, actually had very limited powers when dealing with pollution control and other environmental issues.

Besides the central level, environmental protection bureaus at various local levels are also in a disadvantageous position when performing their duties (Figure 3.3). In all cases, it is the local government, not the higher levels of the environmental protection apparatus, that provides local environmental agencies with their annual budgetary funds, approves institutional promotions and determines increases in personnel and even allocation of resources such as cars, office buildings, and employee housing (Jahiel 1998: 35). Local leaders, including the party bosses and administrative chiefs, all treat economic growth as top priority and are unwilling to see the local economy and investment hampered by implementation of strict environmental regulations. High-speed economic growth not only is an important index of local officials' performances and linked to their future promotion prospects, it also increases local fiscal revenues and benefits local officialdom materially as a whole. China's maintenance of double-digit economic growth in the first decade of the twenty-first century, which was much higher than forecast by the central government in its 10th (2001–05) and 11th Five-Year (2006–10) Plan, had been imposing huge pressures upon natural resources and the ecology.

Since the early 1990s, China's officialdom has formed a culture whereby GDP growth is a major indicator of administrative chiefs' performances and even determines their future promotions. In 2004, the Chinese government started to work on the criteria and indexes of a "green GDP," which deducts the cost of environmental damage and resources consumption from the traditional gross domestic product. In 2007, however, China announced that it would scrap the "Green GDP" report, saying "there is no internationally accepted standard for calculating green GDP" (*Wall Street Journal* 2007). The initiative proved too difficult to continue after the three-year trial period, because it met strong resistance from China's local officials, who have long been rewarded mainly on their ability to improve growth.

Officials at all levels have been aware of the seriousness of China's pollution problems for a long time, but local administration's unitary goal on GDP growth greatly weakened clean-up motivation. It is the job of the EPBs/EPOs to supervise environmental causes, but their heavy dependence upon local government and disadvantaged positions in interaction with other departments made green targets very difficult to achieve. On 23 November 2007, the central government released a

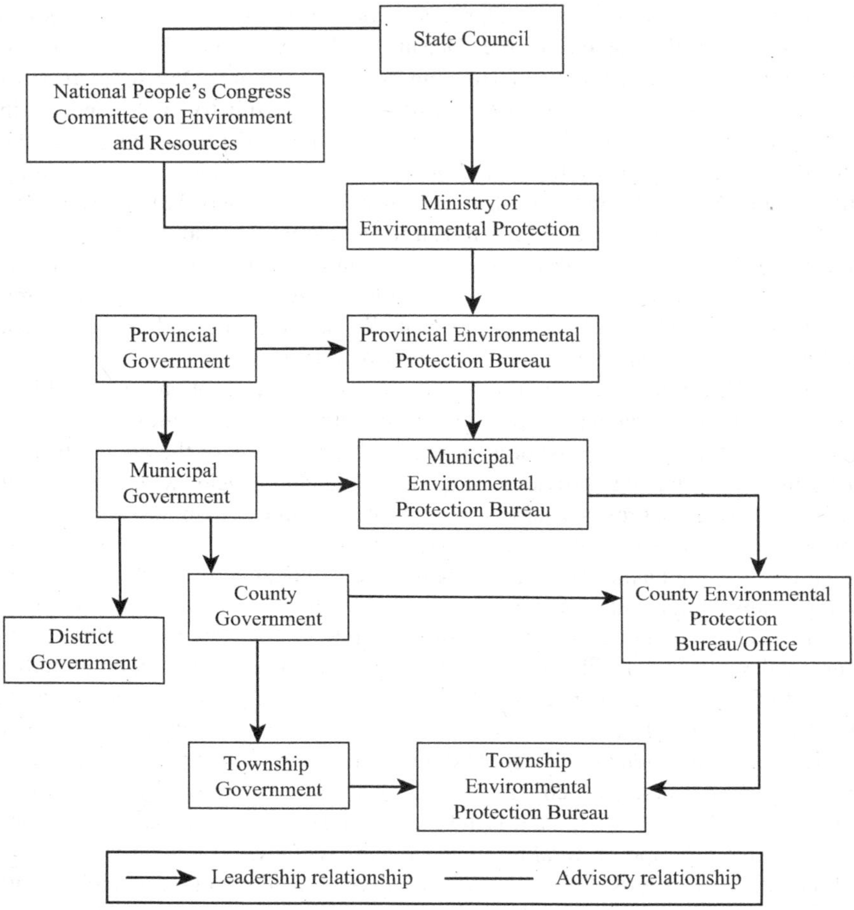

Figure 3.3 China's environmental protection apparatus.

circular that uses green figures of per unit GDP energy consumption and major pollutants reduction to assess provincial officials' performances. Instead of pure economic figures, the Chinese government was trying to measure local officials' achievement through a much more complicated system that also includes environmental indexes. According to the "Implementation Plan for Unit GDP Energy Consumption Assessment System" approved by the State Council and included in the circular, major officials of the provincial-level regions as well as leaders of the top-1000 state-owned or controlled energy consumption enterprises were to be assessed by per-unit GDP energy consumption figures calculated through a quantified scoring methodology. For all provincial governments, energy conservation assessment results would be provided to the personnel department, and would be regarded as an important basis for a comprehensive assessment of the National Leading Group and leading officials of the government. The accountability system and one ballot veto system have been implemented. Within those provincial governments which are evaluated as failing to meet those targets, the leading officials are excluded from the annual award competition and are not considered for any honorary title. The central government will temporarily halt the verification and approval of newly constructed high-energy consuming projects in that region. Those top-1000 key enterprises which are evaluated as failing to meet the targets will be subject to a notice of criticism, and shall not be allowed to attend the annual award competition, or to receive any honorary title or be granted inspection-free and other incentive treatments. The verification and approval of their newly constructed high-energy consuming investment projects and newly added industrial land will be suspended.

The Supervision and Management Agency for State Owned Assets will view the assessment results for sole state-invested or state-holding enterprises as an important basis for the performance assessment of the leaders of those top-1000 key enterprises. The one ballot veto will be implemented. Those provincial governments and top-1000 key enterprises which are evaluated as failing to meet the targets shall be asked to take actions for rectification and upgrading during a given time. For those who fulfilled or surpassed the assessment targets, commendation and awards will be granted.

Facing huge pressures from the central government and the public, local officials had to take high-profile measures, including closing down polluting factories and punishing lower-level officials, but their anxiety about the possible slowdown of economic growth and huge clean-up cost remains. After a time, when public attention becomes distracted, environmental standards and law enforcement will become lax again. This is the vicious circle that prevents localities from taking firm emission-cutting actions. Local, stricter environmental requirements could only drive away entrepreneurs and investors if other regions of China do not adopt similar measures.

Many local EPBs have for years been facing the problem of fund shortage, and some cannot even afford the salaries of their staff. Local environmental agencies therefore retained a portion of the pollution fees and fines they collected from polluters to alleviate the need for funding. As these arrangements might foster corruption and encourage EPBs to focus on collection of pollution fees and fines instead of reducing total pollution, the country decided to reform this revenue retention system by introducing the scheme called "two separate lines for revenues and expenses" (*shouzhi liangtiao xian*). During this nationwide reform, that started in the late 1990s, not only environmental departments, but all kinds of administrative agencies at all levels were required to decouple their revenue from their expense streams in a bid to prevent corruption and promote accountability. In environmental management, all pollution fees and fines now go directly to the local finance bureau, and the EPB is no longer guaranteed a partial refund of their pollution fees (Lo and Tang 2007: 48). Taking Guangzhou City as an example, under the new system, all fees and fines collected become part of the general funds, with 10 percent going to the national treasury, 5 percent to the provincial treasury, and the remaining 85 percent to the municipal treasury (Lo and Tang 2007: 48).

The new system requires EPBs to develop an annual budget, which must be approved by the finance bureaus and then incorporated into the regional budget before submission for parliamentary approval. Different from past practices, in which each bureau collected its own fees and used the funds at its discretion, the new system, to a large extent, has played a positive role in curbing corruption and increasing transparency. For some environmental officials, however, the new system also has a negative impact on the EPB because financial power is now concentrated at the finance bureau and it takes more time and effort for the EPB to request funding (Lo and Tang 2007: 49). From this perspective, the new system has made EPBs more financially dependent upon the local government.

The new system did not solve the funding insufficiency problem effectively in all parts of China. In less-developed regions with limited finances, the funds allocated to local EPBs each year sometimes are far from sufficient to cover the expenses of normal operation. The difference has to be offset by local EPBs themselves through providing some forms of commercial services and retaining a portion of such income while the majority of it is submitted to financial bureaus. In practice, many EPBs still keep about one-third of the pollution fees to make ends meet, although this practice conflicts with the principle of "two separate lines for revenues and expenses." How the revenue–expense separation system has been implemented therefore varies in different localities.

EPB's funding shortage is also partly attributed to the overstaffing problem in local governmental departments. In the EPB of Lingbi County, Anhui Province, the number of formal staff members on the state payroll (*bianzhinei renyuan*) was 21 in 2007 but, in reality, this EPB recruited a total of 94 staff members, with only eight totally reliant on county payment and 13 relying for 70 percent of their salaries on county payment (*People's Daily* online 2007). All the other 73 persons (*bianzhiwai renyuan*) were working for the environmental supervision team (*huanjing jiancha dadui*), with their income utterly dependent upon the EPB instead of the county government. The Lingbi EPB in 2006 collected pollutant discharge fees worth 990,000 yuan, 35 percent of which was retained by the EPB to pay its staff. Despite such practices, which actually conflicted directly with the State Council Regulation on Pollutant Discharge Fee Collection and Use, the average income of staff working in the environmental supervision team was still only a little higher than 200 yuan per month, even lower than the 360 yuan per month minimum salary level set by the Lingbi government. The overstaffing problem is partially due to the rampant nepotism in local government departments, with major county officials putting their relatives and friends into the EPBs and other government agencies. Such severe funding shortage prevents local EPBs from making all-out efforts to decrease total pollutant emissions and instead forces them to focus on collecting pollution fees and fines. With revenue and expenses gradually being separated under the new system, some of these pollution fees and fines may turn into bribes of various forms. If the powers and functions of environmental agencies at various levels are expanded, as suggested by some scholars and experts, corruption involving environmental officials may increase if relevant supervision and monitoring systems are not put in place.

One of the most fundamental causes leading to China's inefficiency in solving ecological problems may lie in the abovementioned multi-sectioned and multi-layered bureaucratic structures in the country. In a state-centric country like China, the government, rather than the market and civil society, plays a dominant role in environmental protection; thus, when the governmental institutions have innate flaws, any green effort that may compromise the economic growth and fiscal revenue will probably encounter insurmountable obstacles.

Who has the final say: China's fragmented energy bureaucracy

Like many other countries, China's response to climate change is intertwined with its energy policy process, in which even the powerful NDRC lacks the authority, resources, and tools to prevail over other state energy oligarchies. For the past 30 years, China has gone through periodic restructurings of its energy bureaucracy and three cycles in its establishment of a central energy agency aimed at ending the splintering of energy sector authority among multiple institutions, but despite the growing importance of energy security on China's domestic and foreign agendas, the country has always failed to establish an authoritative agency over the fractured energy sector, which is currently made up of over a dozen powerful players at the national level. A high-level National Energy Commission headed by two vice premiers was established in 1980 but was abolished only two years later. A Ministry of Energy was established in 1988 but was eliminated in 1993, giving way to market allocation of energy resources (Bo 2010: 1). The low-rank and understaffed Energy Bureau was set up subsequently under the NDRC, which was unable to coordinate effectively across industries and ministries in the formation and enforcement of energy policies. In contrast to the hundreds, if not thousands, of employees working in the energy bureaucracy to make policy and oversee industry in many industrialized nations, only about 30 employees were working at the NDRC's Energy Bureau in China. In recognition of the need to strengthen energy sector management, the government, in 2005, had to establish the National Energy Leading Group under the State Council, an inter-agency coordination panel headed by Premier Wen Jiabao himself. During another round of governmental restructuring in 2008, the National Energy Leading Group was formally restructured as the National Energy Commission (NEC), while the NDRC's Energy Bureau was upgraded to the vice-ministerial level National Energy Administration (NEA). All these bureaucratic restructurings, however, were just "old wine in new bottles" and did not fundamentally change the scattered responsibility and authority among multiple powerful stakeholders. Turf wars among various energy institutions have often resulted in energy laws that fail to specify the agencies responsible for the content of those laws, delaying or preventing implementation, while China's state-owned energy companies, powerful and relatively autonomous thanks to their full or vice-ministerial ranking, are able to initiate major energy projects and policies and sometimes advance corporate interests at the expense of national ones (Downs 2008: 42).

Since the high-profile governmental reorganization in 2008, both the NEA and the Ministry of Environmental Protection have been endowed with more political clout than their predecessors, but still not enough to mediate the bureaucratic infighting that disrupts energy and climate policy making. The heads of some of the politically powerful and relatively autonomous state-owned energy companies – for example, the China National Petroleum Corp. (CNPC), China Petroleum and Chemical Corp. (Sinopec), State Grid Corp., and Shenhua Group – hold ministerial rank (Downs 2008: 43). As successors to the former industrial ministries (such as the Ministry of Petroleum and the Ministry of Electrical Powers) during the period of the command economy, many of these energy giants still witness their executives sitting in the paramount CCP Central Committee and have access to face-to-face discussions with top leadership. The concept of "fragmented authoritarianism" identified by Kenneth Lieberthal in China's decision making (Lieberthal 1992: 1–30) provides a useful lens for viewing the processes of formulating and implementing energy- and climate-related policies. In this fragmentation of authority, all institutions and all individuals of any importance hold a specific rank, and this rank is a critical determinant of the geometry of policy bargaining (Lieberthal and Oksenberg 1988: 142–57). In the days of the planned economy, the large state industries were either ministries or affiliated bureaus so, partly for this reason, the few remaining large state-owned enterprises still retain considerable influence at the highest levels of government (Shirk 1993: 107–15). The state-owned energy companies have proved adept at defining the energy policy agenda (Andrews-Speed 2004: 55), and regulatory agencies like the NEA and the Ministry of Environmental Protection more often than not find themselves in a disadvantageous position when bargaining with those industrial giants on the formulation and implementation of energy and environmental policies. Conflicting objectives within energy policy, let alone between energy policy and other policies (for example, climate-related policy), are thus unavoidable (Andrews-Speed 2004: 54). On the one hand, the state-owned petroleum, coal, hydropower, and nuclear giants all want to increase their production and obtain more subsidies or tax rebates from the government; on the other hand, for the sake of sustainable development and mitigation of climate change, central government has to reduce reliance upon traditional fossil fuels, including coal and petroleum while increasing the share of clean energy like hydropower, wind power, and solar power. Despite widespread recognition among PRC officials and energy experts of the need to make the country's energy institutions effective, growing support for the establishment of a ministry of energy, powerful ministerial and corporate interests favor the status quo, with energy firms being reluctant to have another political manager and fearing that it would limit their direct access to China's leadership (Downs 2008: 45). As China lacks an authoritative regulatory body to resolve disputes among powerful energy giants, their competing and conflicting interests are likely to undermine not only policy formulation and implementation, but also the drafting of energy- and climate-related laws and regulations.

4 Largest beneficiary from carbon trade

The Kyoto Protocol, the first international treaty including detailed obligations for industrialized nations to reduce their greenhouse gas (GHG) emissions by 2012, has, in reality, yielded huge benefits for China instead of imposing afflictive restraint upon the world's fastest-growing economy. China, then the world's second largest GHG emitter after the United States, completed its domestic ratification process in 2002, and appealed to other hesitant parties to ratify the protocol as soon as possible. The Kyoto Protocol came into effect in 2005, requiring 38 industrialized countries to reduce their GHG emissions between 2008 and 2012 by an average of 5.2 percent below 1990 levels. China is not one of the 38 countries named, and it is not required to reduce its GHG emissions. With no compulsory burden to shoulder, China is actually economically incentivized by the Kyoto Protocol to participate in international joint actions against climate change, announcing repeatedly that future international climate talks should continue to follow the pattern set by Kyoto.

CDM profit: low-hanging fruit for China

To attract both developed and developing countries to join the Kyoto Protocol, the protocol introduced a flexible mechanism called the Clean Development Mechanism (CDM). Industrialized nations, such as Japan and Canada, which have difficulties meeting even the minimum requirements set by the protocol, can invest in overseas environmental projects in developing countries that have no emission reduction obligations and then buy certified emission reductions (CERs) to offset their obligations. The CDM encourages industrialized nations to give more fiscal and technological aid to developing countries for environmental protection. As the deadline year of 2012 for industrialized nations' 5 percent emission reduction was approaching, they were in urgent need of buying CERs from developing countries to meet the Kyoto requirement. Even if some of them are able to fulfill the goal on their own, they still have incentives to buy CERs because the emission reduction cost in developing countries is much lower than that seen in developed countries.

China, the largest developing country with the world's largest GHG emissions, enjoys the highest CDM project potential because its marginal cost of emission reduction is relatively low compared to that of many other developing countries.

Experts attribute this to its low technological level and the use of inefficient energy equipment. It is often more difficult and expensive for a project with high standards of technology and modern facilities to cut down emissions as the room for further GHG abatement is already limited. The World Bank estimated that China's CDM project potential could account for half of the world's total. The Organisation for Economic Co-operation and Development (OECD) also reported that most CDM projects would best be operated in China (OECD 1999: 56). Besides fund injection and technology transfer in CDM projects, both Chinese corporations and the government can gain huge profit from the sale of CER to foreign organizations. Expects have predicted that China will become the largest carbon credits provider in global carbon trading by 2012 through CDM projects, which will increase foreign investment in China by about US$475 million in 2010, US$356 million in 2015, and US$238 million in 2020 (Lu and Liu 2004: 133). Although this increase in FDI represents only a small portion of the tens of billions of dollars China attracts each year, the CDM development is a surprising windfall that may have the catalytic effect of replacing outdated installations, promoting public awareness about environmental protection, and solving pollution problems efficiently.

Chinese government's revenue from CDM projects

On 30 June 2004, seven months before the implementation of the Kyoto Protocol, the Chinese government enacted a draft regulation on the management of CDM projects in China, showing that it was prepared and eager to gain from the Protocol. On 12 October 2005, with the amendment of the draft regulation, the National Development and Reform Commission (NDRC), the Ministry of Science and Technology, the Ministry of Foreign Affairs, and the Ministry of Finance jointly issued the Measures for Operation and Management of Clean Development Mechanism Projects in China to replace the draft regulation (Office of the National Coordination Committee on Climate Change and Institute of Nuclear and New Energy Technology of Tsinghua University 2006: 55). According to China's Measures for Operation and Management of Clean Development Mechanism Projects in China, revenue from the transfer of CERs shall be owned jointly by the Government of China and the CDM project owner, with the allocation ratio defined as follows:

a the Government of China takes 65 percent CER transfer benefit from HFC (hydro fluorocarbons) and PFC (perfluorocarbons) projects;
b the Government of China takes 30 percent CER transfer benefit from N_2O project;
c the Government of China takes 2 percent CER transfer benefit from CDM projects in priority areas and forestation projects.

(NDRC 2005: Article 24)

In August 2005, just half a year after the official implementation of the Kyoto Protocol, Japan's JMD Greenhouse Gases Reduction Co. Ltd and the Juhua Co. Ltd, based in east China's Zhejiang Province, agreed to establish a CDM project to help the Chinese firm to reduce nearly 40 million tons of its carbon dioxide equivalent discharges over seven years. The JMD provided all funding and technologies to decompose HFC23 discharged by a chemical plant owned by Juhua. The decomposition of the potent greenhouse gas HFC23 was the so-called "low-hanging fruit" in carbon offset projects. This gas from the perfluorocarbon family of gases is a byproduct of the production of refrigerant gases. It is relatively cheap to deal with, simply being burnt. Yet to do so is a very lucrative activity in global carbon markets because each ton of HFC23 is equivalent to 11,700 ton of carbon dioxide in terms of its global warming impact. So a small amount of HFC23 destruction earns a huge volume of CERs. According to the contract, the JMD would purchase emission credits at a price of at least US$6.5 per ton CO_2 equivalent, which is equal to at least US$36.5 million every year, or a total of US$255.8 million for the seven contractual years based on the anticipated annual reduction of more than 5.62 million tons of carbon dioxide (*Shanghai Securities News* 2006: A7). This became the first large-scale CDM deal in China.

A few months later, another Chinese chemical plant signed an even larger emission-reduction deal with the World Bank. At that time, this was the largest ever CDM project in the world. According to the contract, the Changshu 3F Zhonghao New Chemicals Material Co. Ltd in Jiangsu Province would receive 438 million euros for cutting HFC23 emissions by the equivalent of 10.43 million tons of carbon dioxide annually for the next seven years. These were China's first two large-scale CDM businesses, from which the Chinese government was expected to gain US$385 million selling CERs to international buyers, who can resell the emission permits in the international carbon market to companies and governments that find it difficult to meet the Kyoto Protocol requirement in the 2008–12 period.

The largest share of CDM cake

By 19 July 2011, 3,294 CDM projects worldwide were registered with the United Nations, which were expected to reduce emissions by 494 million tons of carbon dioxide equivalent every year (Figures 4.1 and 4.2). Of them, 1,484 China-based CDM projects were registered with the United Nations, accounting for 45.05 percent of the world's total. By the same date India had 698 CDM projects registered with the United Nations, accounting for 21.19 percent of the total and ranking the second among all developing countries. In terms of CERs being produced per annum, however, the gap between China and India expanded even further because an individual CDM project in China is on average on a much larger scale than an Indian project in producing carbon credits. China hosted about 45 percent of the world's CDM projects, which produced more than 63 percent of the world's total CERs annually, while India had about 21 percent of the world's CDM projects, which could only produce some 10 percent of the world's total CERs (Figures 4.1 and 4.2). China's CDM projects are on average more efficient

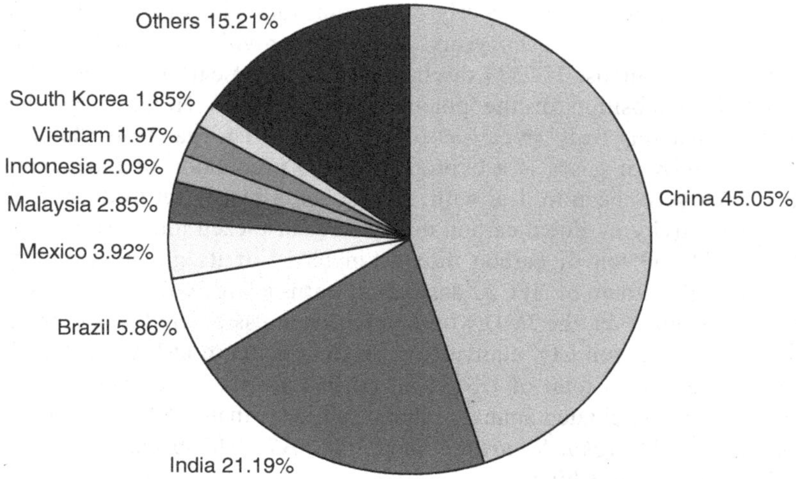

Figure 4.1 Registered CDM projects by host party (total: 3,294).

Source: UNFCCC (2011a).

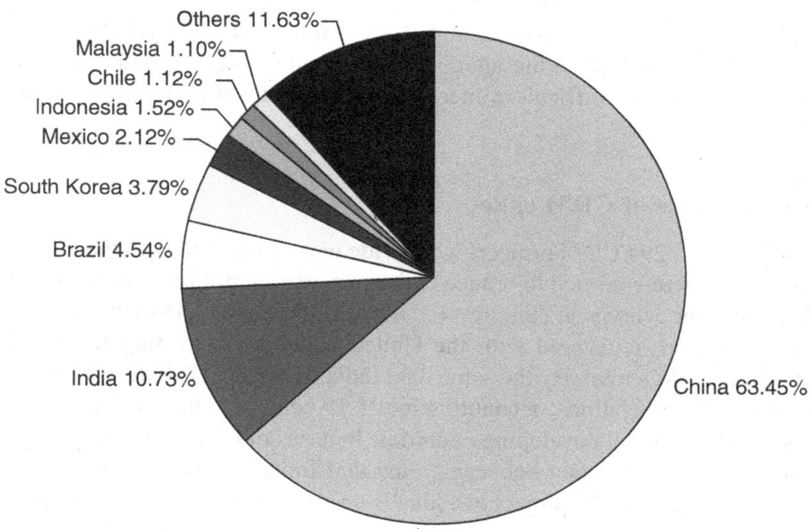

Figure 4.2 Expected average annual CERs from registered CDM projects by host party (total: 494,152,860).

Source: UNFCCC (2011b).

in producing CERs than their peers elsewhere largely because many of the Chinese hosts are good-sized chemical factories that emit such GHG by-products with huge global warming potentials (GWPs) as HFCs and PFCs. In the above-mentioned case of Juhua, the decomposition of HFC23, a GHG that is about 11,700 times more powerful than carbon dioxide in making our planet warm, is a very profitable business in global carbon markets because the destruction of the same quantity of HFC23 earns about 11,700 times more CERs than that of CO_2.

International carbon trade includes both project-based emission reduction deals (under the CDM and Joint Implementation schemes stipulated by the Kyoto Protocol) and direct emission permits transactions (under the Emission Trading scheme stipulated by the Kyoto Protocol). About 90 percent of the total turnover of global carbon trading is contributed by project-based emission deals. Since the Kyoto Protocol took effect in February 2005, the average price of CERs produced by CDM projects has been rising steadily. The possible price rise of carbon credits would probably make China's business more financially attractive. The supply of credits will be 300 million metric tons short of demand when the Kyoto Protocol on reducing pollution expires in 2012, according to a World Bank forecast in 2007 (*Bloomberg News* 2007). From January 2004 to April 2005, the prices of CERs in the international market varied from US$3 to US$7 per ton of CO_2 equivalent (Office of the National Coordination Committee on Climate Change and Institute of Nuclear and New Energy Technology of Tsinghua University 2006: 6). Increased demand had raised the prices of the credits by more than 70 percent from February to May 2007, and Japan paid as much as US$16 per ton of CO_2 equivalent compared with an average price of US$10 in 2006 (*Bloomberg News* 2007). Under the European Union Emission Trading Scheme (EU ETS), the largest multinational, greenhouse gas emissions trading scheme in the world, the carbon price has, for a long time, been above 20 euro per ton CO_2 equivalent. The EU scheme is largely modeled on the mechanisms in the Marrakech Accords of the Kyoto Protocol, helped by the experience gained during the running of the voluntary UK Emissions Trading Scheme in previous years.

Contracted CER prices differ, not only according to the supply–demand relationship in the international carbon market, but also on the basis of the certainty of CDM projects, which are, for the most part, financially risky and technologically complicated. According to UN Regulations, all CDM projects have to follow the principle of "additionality," which means that the projects must demonstrate that the activities would not have occurred under normal technical and economic conditions in the host country without CER revenues.

The rule of "Economic Additionality" requires that the resources from the Annex I investors are in addition to the financial obligations of the Annex I Party under the Convention, and to current official development aid flows. The principle of "Environmental Additionality" requires that the CDM project activity brings about long-term environmental benefits related to the mitigation of climate change that would not have occurred in the absence of the project.

As CDM project developers' profit from selling CERs to international buyers is additional to the original project revenue, the project's IRR (internal rate of return) will be increased with this carbon finance (IRR is a capital budgeting metric used by firms to decide whether they should make investments, and it is an indicator of the efficiency of an investment as opposed to net present value, or NPV, which indicates value or magnitude). This means that some environmentally friendly projects, previously regarded as financially infeasible and not worth investing in, suddenly become profitable after being authorized as a CDM project due to the additional revenue available through selling carbon emission reductions produced by the project.

It is estimated that the IRRs of solid waste management projects can be enhanced by between 5 and 7.5 percent through becoming a CDM project, while those of collective heating supply projects can be boosted by between 2 and 4 percent (Office of the National Coordination Committee on Climate Change and Institute of Nuclear and New Energy Technology of Tsinghua University 2006: 7). The IRRs of biomass projects can go up by between 0.5 and 3.5 percent and the IRRs of wind farm and hydropower projects can increase by between 1 and 2.5 percent after they become CDM projects (Office of the National Coordination Committee on Climate Change and Institute of Nuclear and New Energy Technology of Tsinghua University 2006: 7). Experts in China believe renewable energy and energy-efficiency projects have the greatest potential for expansion in China's carbon market, given China's inefficient energy consumption, favorable government policies, and international technical support. Renewable energy projects are currently not as profitable as traditional power projects in China and elsewhere, so the CDM will generate extra revenue for these projects thus making new green energy more attractive.

Government's attempt to boost CDM projects

The Chinese government has been consulting international organizations, such as the World Bank and the United Nations Development Program (UNDP), as well as the governments of Italy, Canada, France, Japan, and Germany to help local Chinese departments to establish CDM service centers, in order to address the bottleneck of technical services. The Chinese government has been conducting more training activities for officials, senior managers, and consultants to familiarize them with the procedures of CDM projects and to utilize this opportunity to absorb foreign funds and technology.

With the assistance of the UNDP, China is establishing a national CDM fund to offer aid for local projects. The NDRC, the Ministry of Finance, the Foreign Ministry, and the Ministry of Science and Technology will jointly set up an auditing council to take charge of the fund. Active CER buyers in the world include international organizations, government-sponsored fundraising organizations, commercial organizations, and NGOs (non-governmental organizations). The World Bank is now the largest CER buyer, managing a number of carbon funds, including the Prototype Carbon Fund and the Umbrella Carbon Facility, and acting as a trustee of governmental carbon funds in some European countries. The Umbrella Carbon Facility became a CER buyer in a major HFC23 project in east China's Jiangsu Province. The British government encourages its business sectors to actively engage in the CDM market. A CDM promotion section was set up within the Department of Trade and Industry (DTI) of Britain and, in July 2005, the DTI organized a delegation to Beijing, Chongqing, and Guangzhou to promote CDM cooperation and CER purchase. Spain, Sweden, Norway, Austria, Denmark, and Finland have set up agencies for CDM development, allocating a special budget for overseas CDM cooperation. A Japanese Carbon Fund (JCF) was established in December 2004, with a total fund of US$140 million. Canada has also established a climate change fund to support developing countries in their CDM capacity-building activities. In 2005, the Canadian government set aside a huge budget for meeting the Kyoto Protocol requirements, including provision for overseas CDM promotion. Besides organizations and governments of OECD countries that have legal obligations on emission reduction, other governmental agencies, investment funds, and corporations are possible investors in China's CDM projects and buyers of CERs if they want to profit from the CER resale in the international market.

According to Chinese regulations, CDM project developers should be Chinese-funded or Chinese-controlled enterprises in China. China's CDM projects are most likely to occur in its agriculture, forestry, coal, steel and iron, power, chemical, transportation, renewable energy, paper making, machinery manufacture, non-ferrous metallurgy, construction material, and heat supply industries. Due to the absorption of foreign investment and advanced technology in the implementation of CDM projects, scholars expected CDM programs to boost the country's GDP by 0.03 percent in 2010, 0.34 percent in 2020 and 0.52 percent in 2030 (Figure 4.3; Lu and Liu 2004: 133). Although the figure is relatively small at the preliminary stage, the increase is expected to accelerate later on because of the ripple effect of environmental projects on the national economy. In general, the CDM benefits China by:

- financing emission reduction projects;
- bringing China huge profits from selling CERs;
- providing new channels for environmentally friendly technology transfer;
- improving energy efficiency and energy conservation;
- improving local environmental conditions;
- alleviating poverty by increasing income and offering job opportunities.

Industrialized countries' emission reduction obligations under the Kyoto Protocol framework are certain to affect international energy prices, because OECD countries have to restrain their domestic petroleum and natural gas consumption and reduce energy imports. The drop in international petroleum and natural gas prices caused by shrinking fossil fuel demand after the implementation of the Kyoto Protocol will help China save money in the import of oil and gas. With increasing demand for imported petroleum and natural gas, China is very sensitive to

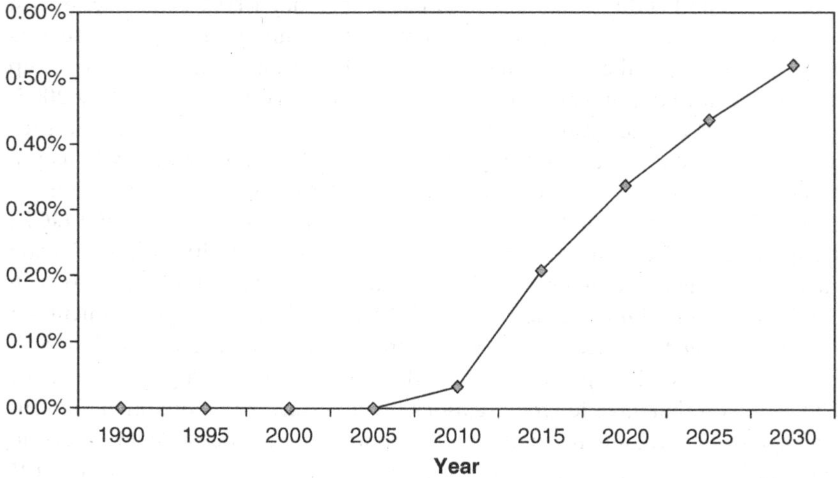

Figure 4.3 Potential CDM benefits as percentage of GDP in China.

Source: Lu and Liu (2004: 133).

international energy price fluctuations. In a short period of time, China has evolved from being an oil exporter in 1992 to being the world's second largest oil importer (only after the United States) in 2008. The emission reduction obligation committed to by many OECD countries will help alleviate China's anxiety about any international energy price hike. The World Bank has estimated that the Kyoto Protocol's emission reduction target will bring down petroleum prices by 10 percent and natural gas prices by 17 percent in 2010 if no emission trading is allowed. Even if emission trading is carried out among industrialized countries, a reduction of petroleum and natural gas prices by 5 percent and 14 percent respectively can still be expected (Ellerman *et al.* 1998: 15).

Procedures of China-based CDM projects

Any CDM project anywhere in the world has to be finally approved by the CDM Executive Board (EB), which was set up by the United Nations Framework Convention on Climate Change (UNFCCC) in 2001. Before submitting their applications to the EB, project developers must navigate their way through a series of complicated procedures and obtain permission from the designated national authority (DNA) in the host country. CDM projects are externally verified and certified by "Designated Operational Entities" (DOEs), third-party organizations designated by the parties to the Kyoto Protocol.

Generally speaking, a typical China-based CDM project has to go through the following stages before it can produce CERs.

Project identification

Project owners and other project participants – including international investors and potential CER buyers from Annex I countries – discuss the feasibility, technology options, fund allocation, and other issues concerning the projects. A project idea note (PIN) can be worked out with a series of factors including the additionality principle, transaction cost, project risk, and the method of funding under consideration.

Project design

After the initial contact and negotiations, project developers must fill out a form of project design document (PDD), which can be downloaded from the UNFCCC's official website. The content of a PDD includes a description of the project, application of baseline methodology, crediting period of CERs produced by the project, calculation of greenhouse gas emission reductions, environmental impact, and opinions from other stakeholders. All projects must conform to China's sustainable development criteria.

Host country's approval

According to *Measures for Operation and Management of CDM Projects in China* (NDRC 2005), the DNA in China is the NDRC. Project initiators should submit their application, including the PDD, to the NDRC for approval. On the basis of the opinions from the National CDM Board, the NDRC approves or rejects the proposal. The Board is co-chaired by the NDRC and the Ministry of Science and Technology (MoST), and also includes members from the Ministry of Foreign Affairs (MoFA), the State Environmental Protection Administration (SEPA), China Meteorological Administration (CMA), and the Ministry of Agriculture (MoA). For each CDM application, it normally takes less than two months to receive a letter issued by the NDRC on the status of the approval.

Project validation

After being approved by the DNA, project initiators should sign a contract with a qualified DOE for future validation. The DOE then starts to examine and appraise the project on the basis of the PDD and other CDM regulations. A validation report should be given by the DOE after the assessment.

Project registration

If the project passes DOE's validation, the DOE will submit the validation report to the EB, applying for project registration. If the application passes the EB's examination, the project will be successfully registered with the United Nations and relevant CERs can be produced by the project.

Project implementation, supervision, and reporting

During the implementation process of the CDM project, project developers are responsible for reporting relevant data concerning emission, baseline, and leakage to the DOE.

Verification and certification of CERs

The DOE examines the supervision report provided by project developers, and verifies the emission reductions produced by the projects by various means, including spot inspection. After verification, the DOE will submit a certification report to the project participants and the EB.

Issue of CERs

After the EB approves the certification application, 2 percent of the CERs will be deposited in a special account as a climate change adaptation fund for least developed countries. The remaining CERs will go into accounts of relevant project participants or parties to the Kyoto Protocol according to the contract.

Challenges and obstacles

China's move to further tap its CDM potential under the Kyoto framework is not without its challenges. Many local corporations still lack the basic knowledge about the Protocol and CDM, or the expertise to prepare PDDs. The complicated application procedures and considerable prophase investment are also obstacles to the launching of CDM projects, which require the approval of both the Chinese government and the United Nations. Project initiators have to ensure that the CER price can cover their additional investment. Many projects concerning environmental protection and system upgrades must employ new equipment and technology, so they sometimes become too risky for commercial banks and other investors.

Most other developing countries, including many very poor ones that are extremely vulnerable to global warming, have been largely left out of the big picture. In 2006, all of Africa received less than US$150 million from selling carbon credits, or 3 percent of the global total (*International Herald Tribune* 2007). The imbalanced regional distribution in carbon trade income, as well as China's surging energy consumption and emissions, have led to international dissatisfaction about the current climate change regime dominated by the Kyoto Protocol. The new round of international talks started at the end of 2007 to formulate a new pact replacing the Kyoto Protocol, and international pressure upon China to bear a compulsory emission cutting onus has been increasing. Environmental activists hope this time, that the United States, the current world number one greenhouse gas emitter, plus China and India, will all be included in the new treaty, with fixed emission quotas or even carbon taxes levied on them.

The United States, the most notable withdrawer from the Kyoto Protocol, refused to accept any mandatory cuts in emissions without a similar commitment from developing countries, notably China.

China is caught in a dilemma. On the one hand, it is concerned about its deteriorating environmental problem, and hopes to utilize international cooperation to solve it; on the other hand, it fears that emission abatement obligations may block its fast economic growth. China's total GDP is less than half the size of the United States', but its total emissions have ballooned to the number one position because of an investment splurge on steel, cement, aluminum, and the like, all hugely energy-intensive industries, plus reliance on coal to produce power. From China's perspective, international effort against climate change is a two-edged sword, which can transfer funding and technology to China, as has already happened, and can also put shackles upon the giant if a disadvantageous pact emerges from future negotiations. Chinese experts argue that if China accepts emission quotas just like those imposed upon industrialized nations in the Kyoto Protocol, it will finally pay much more than it currently gains from CDM projects to buy emission permits from other countries at a higher carbon price in the post-Kyoto period. The alternative carbon tax, if adopted in the next protocol, is expected to cost Chinese industry billions of dollars, at a conservative estimate, if China's economy and emissions continue to grow at current rates.

5 China's efforts to promote clean energy

Amidst increasing global concerns about climate change and energy security, the booming clean energy industry has emerged as one of the major business opportunities of the twenty-first century. In research done by the PEW Charitable Trusts, these clean energy projects include all biomass, geothermal, and wind generation projects of more than 1 megawatt, all hydro projects of between 0.5 and 50 megawatts, all solar projects of more than 0.3 megawatts, all marine energy projects, and all biofuel projects with a capacity of 1 million liters or more per year (PEW Charitable Trusts 2010: 41). The overall investment in clean energy jumped by 230 percent from 2005 to 2009, with installed renewable energy capacity worldwide reaching 250 gigawatts (GW) in 2009, enough to power an estimated 75 million households and equivalent to 6 percent of the world's total (PEW Charitable Trusts 2010: 6–7). China, as a latecomer to modernization, is swiftly emerging as the world's clean energy powerhouse with strong national policies aimed at incentivizing the use of new renewables such as wind and solar power. With clean energy investments up more than 50 percent to US$34.6 billion in 2009, China took the lead among G-20 nations for the first time, pushing the United States into the second place (PEW Charitable Trusts 2010: 15).

Considering the relatively high costs and risks often involved in clean energy production, China's great leap forward in sharpening its competitive edge is closely related to the government's strong support for and heavy subsidies to the newly emerging industry. It is also a natural extension of the country's preferred "no-regret" strategy that emphasizes mitigation actions providing fringe benefits like profitability and employment to the country, regardless of whether or not the threat of climate change is real. For China, such an approach would take as a given that economic growth remains the top priority (Hatch 2003: 55).

Legalized framework on clean energy promotion

With the energy policy being positioned for a long time at the center of its development strategy, China today has formulated some of the world's most ambitious policies and targets to address the dual challenges of global climate change and national energy security. When such renewable energy policies were designed, policy makers may have given more weight to economic factors such as energy supply and jobs rather than environmental care but, in practice, these no-regret policies have been functioning as an efficient means of helping the country to slow down its greenhouse gas growth and gain competitive positions in the clean energy sector. China's parliament, the National People's Congress, enacted the Law on Conserving Energy in 1997, and amended it ten years later in 2007 to make the law stricter under the global context of increasing concerns about climate change. To try to cast off the GDP-centrism that had incurred severe criticism from both intellectuals and the public, the amendment to the Law on Conserving Energy articulated for the first time that the state "will implement a system of accountability for energy conservation targets and a system for energy evaluation whereby the fulfillment of energy conservation targets is taken as one part of the evaluation of local people's governments and their responsible persons" (PRC Amended Law on Conserving Energy 2007: Article 6). In addition, the amendment also promoted the energy conservation policy from the status of "a long-term strategy for national economic development" in the original version to that of "a basic policy of China" (PRC Law on Conserving Energy 2007: Article 4), which is comparable to the policy of family planning that has been strictly implemented for more than 30 years. The amendment required local governments to formulate stricter energy-saving standards than those set by the central government (PRC Amended Law on Conserving Energy 2007: Article 4).

China institutionalized its efforts to develop clean energy capacity by passing the groundbreaking Renewable Energy Law in 2005, which defined renewable energy as non-fossil energy of wind energy, solar energy, water energy, biomass energy, geothermal energy, ocean energy, and so forth (PRC Renewable Energy Law 2005: Article 2). The Renewable Energy Law, together with its amendment, which listed the development of renewable energy as "the preferential area for energy development," introduced new schemes like "cost-sharing," "feed-in tariffs," "mandatory grid-connection," and "renewable portfolio target" systems that had been successful in advancing the cause of renewables in some European nations and US states. The law prompted the government to utilize financial subsidies and tax incentives for the development of renewable energy. Considering the comparable disadvantage of generating electricity from renewable sources, the Renewable Energy Law addressed the core issues of pricing and fee-sharing for on-grid renewable energy through a government-set or government-guided pricing system. Figures showed the cost of electricity generated from solar power at that time was some 3 yuan (40 US cents) per kilowatt-hour, while that from a typical coal-fired power plant was only around 0.22 yuan (2.8 US cents) per kWh (Li 2007). With the stipulation that "grid power price of renewable energy power generation projects shall be determined by the price authorities of the State Council" (PRC Renewable Energy Law 2005: Article 19), the Law required grid companies to "buy the grid-connected power produced with renewable energy within the coverage of their power grid," and to "provide grid-connection service for the generation of power with renewable energy" (PRC Renewable Energy Law 2005: Article 14). To help grid companies to share such costs with end-users, the law allowed grid companies to include grid connection expenses paid by them for the purchase of renewable power and other reasonable expenses in the power transmission cost and recover them from the selling price (PRC Renewable Energy Law 2005: Article 21).

After four years of applying the Renewable Energy Law, the government found that, although the country had rapidly increased its installed capacity of renewable energy, much of this capacity was not promptly connected to the grid and that not all power being generated was being purchased as required by the law. When the Renewable Energy Law was amended in 2009, the top legislature required electricity grid companies to buy all the power produced by renewable energy generators and authorized the State Council energy department, in conjunction with the state power regulatory agency and the State Council finance departments, to determine the percentage of the quantity of electricity generated from renewable energies in the total quantity of electricity generated during the planned period (PRC Amended Law on Renewable Energy 2009: Article 14), a regulation system similar to the Renewable Portfolio Standards (RPS) adopted by some US states. The amendment made it clear that power enterprises refusing to buy power produced by renewable energy generators would be fined up to an amount double that of the economic loss of the renewable energy company (PRC Amended Law on Renewable Energy 2009: Article 29). To encourage grid companies to accept more power generated from renewable sources, the amendment waived the value-added and income taxes levied on grid companies on their revenue (the tax rate is about one-third of the revenue) generated from the surcharge on the retail power tariff for supporting renewable energy (REN21 2009: 20).

Together with those supporting laws and regulations, China has drawn up ambitious plans to increase the proportion of renewable energy (including large hydropower) in the primary energy consumption from 7.5 percent in 2005 to 15 percent in 2020, substituting fossil energy by 400 million tons of coal equivalent and cutting CO_2 discharge by one billion tons and sulfur dioxide discharge by more than seven million tons (Zhang 2005). Excluding hydropower, these renewable energy targets were further broken down by the NDRC as 30 million kW from wind, 30 million kW from biomass, and 1.8 million kW from solar photovoltaic (PV). During the year 2005 when the Renewable Energy Law was first enacted, the utilization of renewable energy including major hydropower in China was equal to 166 million tons of coal equivalent (including large hydropower), accounting for 7.5 percent of China's total energy consumption and equivalent to a saving of 380 million tons of CO_2 emissions (NDRC 2007: 9). Since then, the government itself has been giving large subsidies for cost-sharing in the field of renewable energy development. In the second half of 2008 alone, China distributed 2 billion yuan (US$293 million) in subsidies for power generated by renewable energy sources (*Reuters News* 2009a). As a result of forceful government support, by the end of 2008, China's annual renewable energy use already totaled some 250 million tons of coal equivalent, representing 9 percent of total primary energy consumption (REN21 2009: 7), 1.5 percentage points higher than in 2005.

Incentives and disincentives

Under the framework of Renewable Energy Law and national green targets, detailed institutional incentives and disincentives have been designed by various layers of the government to promote renewable energy development in China. At the national level, the central government has given R&D subsidies totaling 4 billion yuan (US$585 million) for the development and industrialization of core renewable energy equipment, including key components for wind turbines and advanced silicon technologies for solar PV, with another 2 billion yuan allocated for R&D of biofuels (REN21 2009: 20–21). Farmers in remote western regions like Qinghai, Xinjiang, and Inner Mongolia have been receiving subsidies of between 100 and 300 yuan from local governments for the purchase of PV module and small-scale wind turbine systems. As the world's largest market for solar water heating (SWH), China in early 2009 launched a subsidy program for the rural use of electrical household appliances (*jiadian xiaxiang*), including SWH. Since 90 percent of the 30 million households using SWH systems in China were located in urban areas, the subsidy – that covered 17 percent of the appliance cost – gave a strong boost to the popularization of SWH in the less affluent countryside. According to the NDRC's Medium and Long-term Development Plan in 2007, China planned to increase the total installed area for SWH systems to 150 million m^2 by 2010 and 300 million m^2 by 2020 – of this 100 million m^2 will be in rural areas (*AsiaTimes Online* 29 October, 2009). Rural households in western China have also been subsidized for years to use off-grid solar PV systems and small-scale wind energy.

Besides fiscal subsidies, the government has adopted a set of preferential pricing schemes to encourage renewable power generation. Currently, the tariff for wind power is fixed by the NDRC and classified into four levels, as shown in Table 5.1, to give differentiated support to projects located in different regions that vary in local wind resources.

To date, China still has no unified feed-in tariff rate at the national level applied to all the solar PV power projects connected to the grid. Prior to 2009, when the market was small, the approved feed-in tariff rate ranged between four to nine yuan per kWh based on the different characteristics of individual projects (REN21 2009: 22), ten to twenty times that of coal power. The exorbitant cost of producing on-grid solar power, together with enormous cost disparities among projects in various localities, have meant that the government has refused to adopt the fixed feed-in tariff, which policy makers think will lead to over-capacity and costly low-level production in some regions. On some occasions, however, Chinese officials like Ren Dongming, deputy director of the Center for Renewable Energy Development of the Energy Research Institute under the NDRC, have expressed China's readiness to introduce the fixed feed-in tariff only when the conditions have become more settled, with problems of relevant technical limitation and low

Table 5.1 China's regional wind power tariff

Region	*Wind resource*	*Wind power tariff*
Resource Region I	Rich	0.51 yuan/kWh
Resource Region II	Modest	0.54 yuan/kWh
Resource Region III	Modest	0.58 yuan/kWh
Resource Region IV	Low	0.61 yuan/kWh

Source: NDRC (2009b).

Notes

Resource Region I (*yilei ziyuanqu*): Urumqi, Yili, Changji, Karamay, and Shihezi in Xinjiang Autonomous Region and the majority of the Inner Mongolia Autonomous Region excluding Chifeng, Tongliao, Xing'an, and Hulunbeier;

Resource Region II (*erlei ziyuanqu*): Chifeng, Tongliao, Xing'an, and Hulunbeier of Inner Mongolia, Zhangjiakou and Chengde in Hebei Province and Zhangye, Jiayuguan, and Jiuquan in Gansu Province;

Resource Region III (*sanlei ziyuanqu*): Baicheng and Songyuan in Jilin Province, the majority of Xinjiang, excluding Urumqi, Yili, Changji, Karamay, and Shihezi, the whole Ningxia Autonomous Region, most part of Gansu Province excluding Zhangye, Jiayuguan, and Jiuquan and part of Heilongjiang Province;

Resource Region IV (*silei ziyuanqu*): the rest of China excluding the first three resource regions.

efficiency resolved and the wide commercial use of solar PV power achieved, as with wind power. According to Ren, such a fixed feed-in tariff will encourage the influx of foreign capital into the domestic solar PV power industry, and thus increase solar power generation capacity by a large margin (cn.WSJ.com 2010).

Although China's solar power industry is still wrestling with hurdles like high costs, technical difficulties, and low efficiency, the government, in view of the huge potential of the solar industry, has been increasing its subsidies and other incentives for the deployment of large-scale solar PV projects throughout the country. A bidding process for a 10 MW program in the Dunhuang region of western China's Gansu Province resulted in an on-grid price of 1.09 yuan per kWh in 2009. Such a price level is applicable to local projects in surrounding regions with similar solar resources and equipment. One year later, in April 2010, the NDRC announced that four solar power stations in western Ningxia Autonomous Region would adopt a new price level of 1.15 yuan per kWh (cn.WSJ.com 2010), higher than that applied to the Dunhuang program, the first large-scale solar power generation program to be commercialized in China. More significantly, the Chinese government kicked off the unprecedented national "Golden Sun" program in July 2009 with financial incentives and strong R&D support for the installation of at least 500 MW of utility-scale solar PV projects during the period 2009 to 2011. The Chinese Ministry of Finance announced that it would subsidize 50 percent of the costs of building demonstration solar power projects and transmitting and distributing the solar power from those projects. In remote areas that lack the infrastructure to connect to the grid, the incentive will go up to 70 percent for solar PV projects. Under the Golden Sun program jointly launched by the

Ministry of Finance, Ministry of Science and Technology and National Energy Administration, grid companies are required to buy all surplus electricity output from solar power projects that generate primarily for the developers' own needs, at similar rates to benchmark on-grid tariffs set for coal-fired power generators (*Reuters News* 2009b). The Golden Sun program, the most concrete form of policy support for PV projects at the national level so far, sets a cap of 20 MW for each province, requiring those projects qualified for the subsidies to have a generating capacity of more than 300 kilowatt peak, while construction will have to be completed in one year and operations will have to last for at least 20 years. Considering the high cost of operating the current systems, however, even the national subsidy offered by the program is not enough to ensure a reasonable return on investment, so regional and local governments still need to provide an additional subsidy for solar PV developers to cover the shortfalls. To date, not many provincial and municipal governments have announced their detailed plans to supplement the national subsidy in this area. To further boost the development of solar energy, the government has been advised to introduce a nationwide feed-in tariff subsidy for large-scale PV projects after the implementation of the Golden Sun program, but with the problems of low efficiency and excessive governmental expenses in mind, policy makers have not yet fixed on the timing and details of the feed-in tariff.

Since the beginning of 2009 China's central government has subsidized purchases of clean-energy vehicles for public fleets in 13 cities to help the automobile industry develop green technology (*Reuters News* 2009c). The scheme promotes the use of electric, hybrid, and fuel-cell vehicles by public transport operators, taxi firms, and postal and sanitary services in cities such as Beijing and Shanghai. Subsidies will be based on the gap in prices between more energy-efficient vehicles and those with traditional engines, and local governments were asked to allocate money to build and maintain facilities for the green vehicles. With strong support from the government, major state-owned automobile makers announced ambitious plans to enhance research and development in clean-energy vehicles. SAIC Motor Corp, China's biggest automobile maker, said it would set up a venture with a 2 billion yuan (US$293 million) investment to develop hybrid and electric vehicles.

The development and potential of China's clean-energy industry

The government's decisive actions to support and subsidize clean-energy industry have received remarkable paybacks. As the result of the Renewable Energy Law (2005), the Medium- and Long-Term Development Plan for Renewable Energy (2007), and other detailed implementation regulations, China's renewable energy industry has been booming as a new engine of economic growth. Having taken a leading global position in the sector of renewable energy, China is now the world's largest maker of wind turbines and solar panels, as well as the largest producer of wind power (see Table 5.2). Compared to other clean-energy industries, wind

Table 5.2 Top five wind power producers by total capacity (December 2010)

Country	*Capacity (in GW)*	*Percentage of world total*
China	44.73	22.7
USA	40.18	20.4
Germany	27.21	13.8
Spain	20.68	10.5
India	13.07	6.6

Source: Global Wind Energy Council (2011: 12).

power is sufficiently mature to be widely commercialized with modest government subsidies and is now China's fastest developing sector in the field of renewable energy. The Chinese market more than doubled its capacity from 12 GW in 2008 to 25.8 GW in 2009 and added 18.9 GW in 2010 to reach 44.7 GW at the end of 2010. China surpassed India in 2008, and Spain and Germany in 2009, to become the world's second largest wind power producer by the end of 2009. China added a staggering 18.9 GW of new capacity in 2010, thus overtaking the United States to become the world's leading wind power country (Global Wind Energy Council 2011: 10–12). By 2020, wind power will probably surpass nuclear power as China's third-largest source of electricity, after thermal and hydropower (*China Daily Online* 2009a).

China's abundant inland and offshore wind energy resources provide enormous potential for large-capacity wind farms. As a latecomer in the utilization of wind power, China's wind power installed capacity increased at a much slower rate than the world's average level before 2004 but, even during that early stage, strong policy support played a vital role in promoting wind power generation and turbine manufacture. Prior to 1994, there were only a few demonstration wind farms fully financed by the government and, from 1994 to 2003, in-grid wind power was first developed as a new energy source for electrical power generation in China (Yang and Pan 2010a: 5). To import technology from foreign companies and to establish a high-quality Chinese wind turbine generator sector, the former State Development and Planning Commission (SDPC), predecessor of NDRC, initiated the "Ride the Wind Program" (*chengfeng jihua*) in 1996, leading to the establishment of two joint ventures, NORDEX (Germany) and MADE (Spain), which effectively introduced 600 kilowatts wind turbine generator manufacturing technology into China (Ecoworld 2008). The landmark policy came in 2003 when the NDRC launched the "Wind Power Concession Program" (*fengdian texuquan xiangmu*) to build large-capacity wind farms and achieve economies of scale through reducing the in-grid wind power tariff. Under the program, the power grid company signs a long-term power-purchase agreement with the wind power project investor and agrees to purchase the prescribed amount of electricity generated by the project, whose capacity must reach 100 megawatts. Investors and developers of wind farms are selected through a competitive bidding process that determines the in-grid tariff. All end-users of the grid's electricity share the tariff increase due to wind power purchase. As incentives, the government waves the import customs tariff and value-added tax on the equipment and accessories. The "Wind Power Concession Program" that minimizes the risks to investors through government-guaranteed power-purchase agreements has pushed China's wind power industry into a fast-growing stage between 2005 and 2009 when the country's installed wind power capacity more than doubled annually in the four years. By the end of 2005, China had built 59 wind farms with 1,854 wind turbine generators and a 1,266 megawatt in-grid wind power installed capacity, ranking it at number ten globally. In 2009, China's installed wind power capacity reached 25.81 GW, about 20 times that in 2005 and ranking number two after the United States. From 1997 to 2004, however, China's installed wind power capacity maintained only a relatively low level of growth rate, fluctuating between 16.3 percent and 28.4 percent (Yang and Pan 2010a: 6).

China is rich in wind energy resources and has great potential for wind power generation. Figures from the China Meteorological Administration (CMA) showed that China's potential wind energy resources on land, measured at 50 m above ground level, are about 2,380 GW (CMA 2010). The wind-rich areas in China can be grouped into three "wind belts," namely the long coastal belt covering Shandong, Jiangsu, Shanghai, Zhejiang, Fujian, Guangdong, Guangxi, and Hainan Province, the northern belt including northwestern Gansu, Xinjiang and Ningxia Province, northern Inner Mongolia and Hebei Province, and northeastern Liaoning, Jilin and Heilongjiang Province, and the inland belt that covers regions with special geological and topographic characters (NDRC 2008: 21–22). Inner Mongolia alone accounts for about one-third of China's total installed wind power capacity. In addition, it is estimated that, in the 5–20 m deep sea belt along the eastern coastal areas, 700 GW of wind energy potential can be exploited based on the assessment of wind resources at 10 m height, which may provide vital and sustainable energy for the affluent provinces in East China that lack indigenous fossil fuel supplies. China plans to get 20 percent of its electricity from renewable sources by 2020, with some 100 GW of wind capacity and 1.8 GW of solar.

Besides the sharp increase in renewable energy capacity, China today has also become a formidable manufacturer of all kinds of renewable energy equipment. China has vaulted past competitors in Denmark, Germany, Spain, and the United States to become the world's largest manufacturer of wind turbines, and it has leapfrogged the West to emerge as the world's largest manufacturer of solar panels. Meanwhile China is pushing equally hard to build nuclear reactors and the most efficient types of coal power plants. These efforts to dominate renewable energy technologies and equipment raise the prospect that the West may someday trade its dependence on oil from the Middle East for a reliance on solar panels, wind turbines, and other equipment manufactured in China (Bradsher 2010). Multinational corporations are responding to the rapid growth of China's market by building big, state-of-the-art factories in China. Vestas of Denmark has erected the world's biggest wind turbine manufacturing complex in northeastern China, and transferred the necessary technology to build the latest electronic controls and generators. According to the government-backed Chinese Renewable Energy Industries

Association, renewable energy industries in China are creating jobs rapidly, reaching 1.12 million in 2008 and climbing by 100,000 a year (Bradsher 2010).

Challenges and problems

China's burgeoning environment industry faces serious problems of overcapacity and latent financial risks in this round of investment frenzy in the green market. Concerns about a national wind and solar bubble are mounting, while billions of dollars are being pumped into renewable sectors. China's commitment to renewable energy is expensive. Although costs are falling steeply through mass production, wind energy is still 20 to 40 percent more expensive than coal-fired power. Solar power is still at least twice as expensive as coal. Experts worry that, without state assistance or more favorable policies, many large-scale projects will not be profitable and may end up with huge losses or even in bankruptcy.

In terms of wind power development, China often faces the bottleneck problem of connecting its impressive wind power capacity to the national transmission power grid. Even with the "mandatory grid connection" and "renewable portfolio target" schemes institutionalized by the powerful Renewable Energy Law, oligarchic grid companies are still in an advantageous position when bargaining with numerous power plants across the country where not all power generated can be transmitted. The conflict between the grid companies and electricity generation sectors (*wangdian zhizheng*) had been entrenched long before the booming of clean energy, which has led to a huge efficiency loss on the supply side and low prices of electricity sold by power plants to grid companies. Meanwhile, most wind turbines are installed in remote areas too far away from the transmission grid and energy-intensive urban areas. It is estimated that about 30 percent of installed wind capacity in China is lying idle and not connected to the power grid (Forbes 2009). Thanks to the government's generous subsidies and local governments' relentless pursuit of GDP, overinvestment and overcapacity exist in both the wind power generation sector and wind turbine manufacturing. In just a few years, stimulated by forceful government support and attractive state subsidies, China's wind power capacity and related component manufacturing and turbine assembling sectors have undergone massive expansion with signs of overheating. As the province with the richest wind resources in China, Inner Mongolia's installed wind power capacity approached 11.4 GW by March 2011, accounting for at least 30 percent of the nation's total; however, a large portion of the electricity generated there could not be transmitted elsewhere, which has caused huge losses of local wind mills (sina.com news 2011). For many large-scale wind farms located in remote western areas that are rich in wind power, the only chance of profit comes from state subsidies under the country's new energy strategy. If the government reduces its support considerably, both turbine installation and the sale of electricity to the grid may turn out to be loss-making and unsustainable businesses. As a result of a "Buy Chinese" policy to favor local manufacturers, many wind turbine manufacturers have entered the sunrise industry with insufficient technology or capital. Among the 80 major Chinese wind turbine producers, only 10 are capable of annual batch production of over 100 units. The remaining 70 manufacturers accounted for only 2.3 percent of the total market share in terms of new installed capacity in 2008 (Yang and Pan 2010a: 16).

Challenges facing China's solar PV industry come from both the supply side and demand side, with over-subsidy and overinvestment having caused serious overcapacity in the industry. In the second half 2009, China had 80,000 tons of multi-crystalline silicon production facilities under construction, posing a severe potential overcapacity when China's actual annual demand for such key material in the PV power industry was 25,000 to 30,000 tons. Known as the asymmetrical problem of Both-Ends-Out (*liangtou zaiwai*), China imported 95 percent of its PV raw materials due to a lack of advanced technologies producing crystalline silicon and exported 95 percent of its finished products due to an underdeveloped domestic market (Li 2010: 38). In the solar PV industrial chain that includes production of crystalline silicon, silicon ingot and wafer, solar cells, modules and arrays, China can only manufacture 18 percent of global silicon material in the upstream while it accounts for 47 and 54 percent of global production capacity respectively for cells and modules in the downstream (Yang and Pan 2010b: 14). Meanwhile, the high energy consumption and emission of poisonous waste in the production of high purity polycrystalline silicon have cast doubts on an industry labeled as green. Owning rich silicon reserves, China has witnessed a boom in silicon manufacturers and hence a production surge driven by substantial profits, but pollution and energy guzzling in the processing of silicon purification have forced the government to enact directives to discourage the low-level replication of such production lines. In the long run, the overdependence on overseas markets increases the vulnerability of China's PV industry as declining foreign demand may become a major constraint to its development.

6 Controversial alternatives: great leap forward in hydro and nuclear energy

As in many other countries, the electric power sector is vital in order for China to run its modern economy, with fossil fuels providing the bulk of the energy needed to generate electricity. Now, with growing concerns about climate change and power shortage, hydropower and nuclear power, despite being more environmentally controversial than other renewables like wind, solar, and geothermal energy, have been perceived by China as clean alternatives to conventional fossil fuels in a low-carbon-electricity scenario. With a historical lag in the country's nuclear and hydro power sectors, China has been formulating the world's most ambitious policies with enormous investment in place to foster the aggressive construction of new hydropower and nuclear plants, in addition to its impressive input in such established renewable energies as wind and solar power. Compared with other democracies, the authoritarian one-party regime in China faces much less resistance from civil society when pushing forward those hydropower and nuclear mammoths that may pose potentially serious threats to the local ecology. To meet its voracious electricity demand that increases in step with the breakneck economic growth of about 10 percent per annum, China does not really have many environmentally sound and safe choices in such a carbon-constrained era if both the hydro and nuclear options are excluded. After decades of cost-benefit calculations and argumentation, the Chinese government has made the decision to ignore most of the objections and carry on the hydropower and nuclear power renaissance that it believes will provide a good low-carbon solution to the urgent bottleneck problem in power supply.

Hydropower fervor after temporary slowdown

As an attractive solution to address climate change and energy shortage due to their negligible carbon emissions and low operating costs, hydroelectricity projects have long been favored by China, which has the largest number of big dams and the largest installed hydropower capacity in the world (see Figure 6.1). Haunting concerns over the negative ecological and social impact of massive dams, however, have in the past five years, made the government more cautious about hydropower and thus slowed down the construction of such projects.

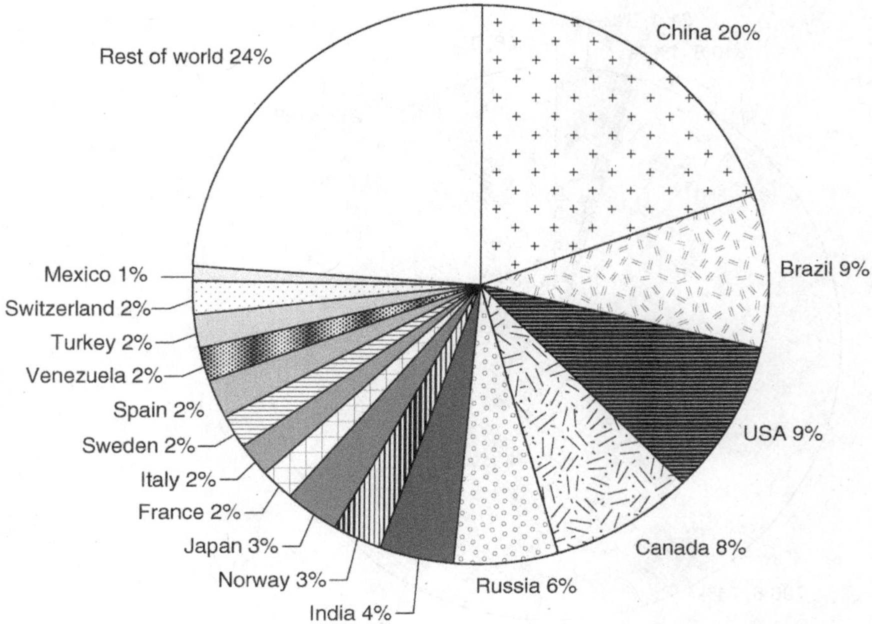

Figure 6.1 Distribution of installed hydropower capacity at the end of 2008.

Source: World Energy Council (2010: 288).

The year 2011, the beginning of the 12th Five-Year Plan (2011–15), witnessed the government's renewed enthusiasm for large hydropower projects, with enormous funds for investment in the construction of environmentally controversial dams and an ad hoc Energy Five-Year Program to formally prioritize the development of hydropower among various forms of power generation (*China Daily Online* 2011). In an effort to help the government boost the share of non-fossil fuels in national energy consumption, China in the next few years will invest 400 billion yuan (US$62 billion) in the construction of four huge hydroelectric dams on the Jinsha River, a tributary of the Yangtze River, according to a report released by the state-owned China Three Gorges Corporation (*China Daily Online* 2011). The total installed capacity of the four dams will be 43 million kilowatts (kW), and is expected to be double that of the Three Gorges Dam, the world's largest power station and China's largest construction project since the Great Wall. By the end of 2010, China's installed hydropower capacity was 213.4 gigawatts (GW), accounting for 22.2 percent of its total installed capacity in power generation that stood at 962.2 GW (Figure 6.2) (China Electricity Council 2010). However, were it not for strong opposition from an environmentally conscious civil society against massive dams, the share of hydropower in the total installed capacity would have been much larger.

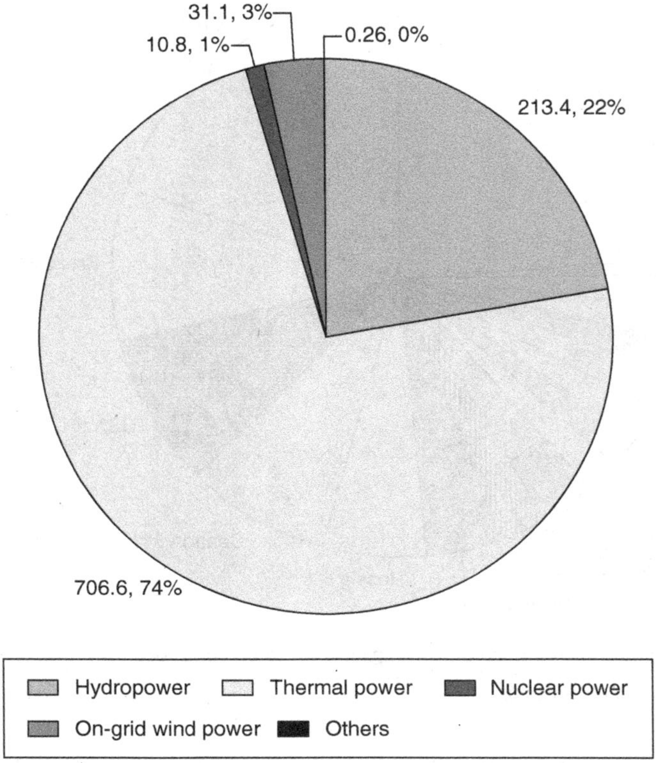

Figure 6.2 Existing installed capacity of various electricity sectors in China by 2010 (gigawatts).

Source: China Electricity Council (2010).

During the 11th Five-Year Plan period (2006–10), the newly established installed hydropower capacity was only a little more than 20 GW, well below the 70 GW increase targeted by the Plan. As a step to change the stagnant development of hydropower and raise the share of non-fossil fuel to at least 15 percent in China's energy mix by 2020, the government has decided to add a staggering 120 GW in installed hydropower capacity from 2011 to 2015, or more than 50 percent of the existing total hydro capacity (ifeng.com news 2011). China's decision to resume the Great Leap Forward in hydropower actually came when the government was freezing the approval of new nuclear plants after the Japanese Fukushima nuclear crisis occurred, providing a wake-up call in March 2011. As low-carbon alternatives to conventional fossil fuels, nuclear and hydropower have been competing with each other for years, with nuclear taking an advantageous position when controversies over the operating Three Gorges Dam made headlines in the past three years. China is building about 28 nuclear reactors, or

Table 6.1 Countries with largest economically exploitable hydro capabilities and percentage being utilized at the end of 2008

Country	*Economically exploitable capability (in TWh/year)*	*% being utilized*
China	1,753	33
Russia	852	21
Brazil	818	45
Canada	536	70
India	442	26
USA	376	68

Source: World Energy Council (2010: 295–307).

roughly 40 percent of the world's total under construction, and the central government has fast-tracked approvals in the past two years (*Reuters News* 2011). The nuclear disaster in Fukushima, however, has dramatically shifted public opinion in favor of hydropower in China.

With large land mass and watersheds, China still has a huge potential for developing its economically and commercially feasible hydro resources, as compared with other advanced hydropower-rich countries like Norway, Japan, and Canada where more than 60 percent of the economically viable hydro resources have already been tapped (Araujo *et al.* 2009: 332). China has the largest economical hydro potential in the world, but only about one-third has been utilized (Table 6.1).

The Chinese government is doomed to face mounting pressure from both home and abroad when it resumes the hydropower leapfrogging that may spark massive relocation of residents, as well as provoking landslides and earthquakes in the surrounding areas in addition to adverse ecological consequences, including water pollution, sediment increase and the blocking of fish migration along the rivers. The State Council has yielded to public concern over the problematic Three Gorges Dam through admitting unforeseeable "urgent problems" faced by the world's biggest hydropower plant (*Guardian* 2011). China's construction of a huge dam over Brahmaputra river in Tibet has irked New Delhi, which earlier expressed its grave concern over the hydropower project that may hinder the Brahmaputra River flowing from Tibet into India (*Zeenews* 2010). Activists from Thailand, Laos, Cambodia, and Vietnam have blamed Chinese dams on the Mekong River for contributing to a drop in river flow and producing irreversible change to the river's ecology (*BBC News* 2010).

Why China prioritizes hydropower

China's electricity output has been growing at an annual rate of about 10 percent (Figure 6.3), on a par with its average economic growth in the past decade. Power shortage and low-carbon commitment have forced China, the world's top energy consumer and carbon emitter, to pay enormous attention to hydropower, nuclear power, and wind power as feasible alternatives to conventional energy like coal and petroleum. China has been facing the headache of power shortage for years, with frequent blackouts disrupting vibrant industrial activities and urban life in many parts of the country. In the context of global climate change, China needs to change the inherent structural problem in its energy mix, i.e. about 70 percent of the country's primary energy consumption comes from coal, which is inherently more polluting and more carbon-intensive than oil and gas.

Compared with other low-carbon energies, hydropower projects serve multiple purposes, including flood control and irrigation, making them more valuable than a single-purpose powerhouse, particularly in vast continental countries like China. China's major river basins are well within the monsoon zone of the Pacific, with over 50 percent of annual precipitation in most areas concentrated in the four months of June to September. Sometimes more than 70 percent of regional rainfalls are concentrated in the two months of July and August. While two-thirds of China's land is threatened by floods and tropical typhoons ravage coastal areas seven times a year on average, hinterland droughts occur almost every year in the dry seasons. Frequent devastating floods have justified the Chinese government's establishment of gigantic dams, such as the Gezhouba Dam and the Three Gorges Dam in the upper reaches of the Yangtze River. Regarded as a solution to both flooding and energy shortage, the building of hydroelectric dams and reservoirs has gradually become commonplace after 1950 and today China has more than 20,000 dams over 15 m high, the largest number of dams in the world (Owen 2011). Taking the Three Gorges Dam as an example, it not only can generate more electricity yearly than all of Japan's hydro stations put together, but also reportedly has amazing flood-control capacity that can withstand the worst flood in 100 years and has played a significant role in improving navigation conditions and increasing shipping capacity along the Yangtze River.

Except for the considerable front-loaded investment associated with hydro stations, hydroelectricity is basically a cheap form of energy, with extremely low operating costs and essentially zero fuel costs, which do not escalate over time as is the case with fossil-fueled resources. If hydro reservoirs are of significant size, they can be used for peaking, intermediate, or base load, greatly increasing their economic advantage and their operational flexibility (Araujo *et al.* 2009: 337). The Japanese Fukushima crisis in 2011 has dramatically shifted public opinion away from nuclear to hydropower in China. China is building about 28 nuclear reactors, or roughly 40 percent of the world's total under construction, but it has frozen the approval of new nuclear plants in the wake of the Fukushima disaster. The world's hydropower capacity under construction at the end of 2008 totaled 171 GW, of which China accounted for 47 percent, or 80 GW, with such massive plants in hand as Xiluodu (12.6 GW), Xiangjiaba (6 GW), Longtan (6.3 GW), Jinping II (4.8 GW), Xiaowan (4.2 GW), Laxiwa (4.2 GW), Jinping I (3.6 GW),

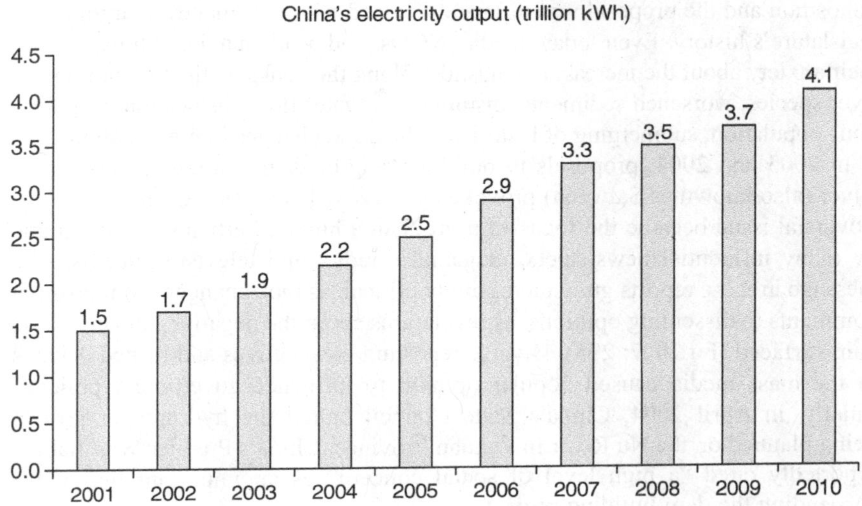

Figure 6.3 China's electricity output, 2001–2010.

Source: National Bureau of Statistics of China (2010).

Pubugou (3.6 GW), Dagangshan (3.6 GW), and Goupitan (3 GW) (World Energy Council 2010: 304–07 and 315).

Despite controversies over large dams and a temporary slowdown in hydropower expansion, the Chinese government has made it clear in the 12th Five-Year Plan (2011–15) that it is to increase investment by large increments so as to add newly installed hydro capacity of 120 GW during the period, or six times more than the increased installed hydropower capacity of 20 GW in the previous five years. China's hydropower expansion is an essential part of its strategy to increase the share of non-fossil sources in the energy mix. To serve the dual purposes of increasing power supply and reducing carbon emissions, China has announced an increase in non-fossil sources to 15 percent of the energy mix by 2020, to 20 percent by 2030 and to one-third by 2050.

Controversies over massive dams and the hydropower slowdown

Long-standing concerns associated with the impact of large dams on ecology, geology, and the displacement of people have been the major barriers confronting China's hydropower ambitions. The construction of the gigantic Three Gorges complex, which is one-and-a-half miles wide and 610 feet tall, has provoked a long-lasting debate over the pros and cons of this largest-ever hydropower project. In 1992, when the then Chinese Premier Li Peng submitted a proposal for the Three

Gorges Dam to the normally pliant National People's Congress, it ran into serious opposition and the proposal was ultimately passed with the smallest margin in the legislature's history. Even today, media, NGOs, and academia are still expressing their anxiety about the increasing landslides along the banks, extinction of migrant river species, worsened sediments, disruption of water flow, dislocation of indigenous population, submerging of historical relics, and changes in precipitation.

In 2003 and 2004, proposals to build a string of dams on the southwest Nu River (also known as Salween) provoked a fierce debate inside China. This controversial issue became the focus of more than a hundred articles and programs by many influential newspapers, magazines, radio, and television outlets. The message in these reports grew increasingly critical, as they changed from positive comments to dissenting opinions, as revelations about the negative impacts of the dam surfaced (Fu 2007: 295). Diverse reporting perspectives and heated debates in the mass media caused popular opinion to influence government policies. Finally, in April 2004, China's State Council halted the hydropower project being planned on the Nu River in Yunnan Province. China's Premier Wen Jiabao, reportedly cited "a high level of social concern" as an important reason for suspending the dam-building project.

China's construction of massive dams and reservoirs on the upstream parts of international rivers has also irked its neighbors. India has expressed its grave concern over the Chinese hydropower project on the Brahmaputra River in Tibet, which may divert the Brahmaputra River flowing from Tibet into India. Activists from Thailand, Laos, Cambodia, and Vietnam have blamed Chinese dams on the Mekong River for contributing to the drop in river flow and producing irreversible change to the river's ecology. Actually, many parts of the world have been more cautious in approving large hydropower stations due to their adverse environmental, ecological, and social impacts. On a global scale, the relative share of hydropower declined from 21 to 16 percent in electric power generation from 1973 to 2004 (International Energy Agency 2006: 24). In California, as in many other places, large hydro resources with capacity larger than 5 MW are distinguished from small hydro; the former is considered environmentally undesirable, the latter acceptable (Araujo *et al.* 2009: 336).

Stringent criticism over densely distributed dams has forced the government to decelerate hydro expansion in the 11th Five-Year Plan period (2006–10), when the newly-established installed hydropower capacity was only a little more than 20 GW, well below the 70 GW target set by the government. The approval of gigantic hydropower stations along torrential rivers like Jinsha River and Nu River was suspended by the central government due to objections from indigenous people and environmental activists.

China's hydropower prospect

China's insatiable demand for energy means that any hydro slowdown is temporary. Rejecting concerns that massive dams are threats to the local environment and people, the central government has planned to add another 120 GW in installed hydropower capacity from 2011 to 2015, or more than 50 percent of the existing total hydro capacity, with super-large projects being prioritized. Some suspended hydropower projects like the Jinanqiao Hydro Station on the Jinsha River have got approval from Beijing. Although China already has the most massive dams and largest installed hydropower capacity in the world, the country, with large land mass and many torrential rivers, still has huge hydro potential to tap compared with other advanced hydropower-rich countries like Norway, Japan, and Canada where more than 60 percent of the economically viable hydro resources have been developed.

China has the largest economical hydro potential in the world, but only about one-third has been utilized. By the end of 2010, China's installed hydropower capacity only accounted for 22.2 percent of its total installed capacity in power generation, much less than some leading countries with the highest percentage of hydropower in the electricity generation. Norway and Brazil rely for more than 80 percent of their power generation from hydropower sources. Despite the government's open statement that the Three Gorges Dam has pressing geological, human, and ecological problems, there is no evidence that such concern would further decelerate hydro expansion in the next five to ten years, as it did in the previous five years. "To increase water-power generation is still the priority for the power industry," said Ouyang Changyu, deputy secretary-general of the China Electric Council (*China Daily Online* 2011). Contrary to the global trend that focuses on small hydro, China will still be interested in mega-projects, with 400 billion yuan (US$62 billion) to be invested in the next few years in the construction of four huge hydroelectric dams on the Jinsha River, a tributary of the Yangtze River. The total installed capacity of the four dams will be 43 GW, and is expected to be double that of the Three Gorges Dam.

It usually takes at least six years to complete the construction of a massive hydropower station, so many of the mega-projects approved or to be approved will not be operational until the end of 2015. The Xiluodu (12.6 GW) and Xiangjiaba (6 GW) hydropower stations on the Jinsha River are likely to be the early birds that can generate electricity within the next two years (Table 6.2). China's burgeoning wind and solar sectors could witness their expansion reducing in the coming five years as the government focuses on cheaper hydropower. Because of wind and solar power's high generating costs and weak competitiveness, their development would be curtailed.

Despite the government's preference for hydropower construction, China's differentiated power pricing system is not in favor of operational hydro powerhouses. Coal-burning power plants are rewarded with higher grid feed-in tariffs than hydropower stations, while wind power prices are even higher and solar power prices the highest. If the government raises feed-in rates for hydropower projects in the near future, that would be a financial incentive to further boost hydro development.

Table 6.2 China's major hydropower projects (completed and under construction) and their (projected) installed capacity

Ranking	*Name*	*Province*	*Installed capacity (GW)*
1	Three Gorges	Hubei	22.4
2	Xiluodu	Yunnan and Sichuan	12.6
3	Baihetan	Yunnan	12.0
4	Wudongde	Yunnan and Sichuan	7.5
5	Longtan	Guangxi	6.3
6	Xiangjiaba	Yunnan and Sichuan	6.0
7	Nuozhadu	Yunnan	5.85
8	Jinping II	Sichuan	4.8
9	Xiaowan	Yunnan	4.2
10	Laxiwa	Qinghai	4.2

Source: author's compilation.

China's nuclear power spree

Nuclear power is the use of nuclear fission reactions to generate electricity for civilian purposes. As an environmentally controversial energy that represents about 15 percent of the world's electricity-generating capacity, nuclear power is believed by some to provide a good path to a low carbon-electricity future (Rothwell and Graber 2009: 176–79) despite safety concerns caused by previous radiation accidents, such as the Three Mile Island accident in 1979 and the Chernobyl disaster in 1986. In comparison to other forms of renewable energies, such as wind power and solar PV, nuclear power generation operates at nearly full capacity and incurs a lower cost that is similar to, or even lower than, traditional coal-fired power generation. Nuclear power plants can be built close to centers of demand, and thus save long-distance power transmission costs. In the case of China, nuclear power is especially important for coastal areas remote from coal fields and where the economy is most vibrant.

Since China decided to build nuclear power plants in the 1970s, it has put 14 nuclear power reactors in operation with a generating capacity totaling 11.3 GW by July 2011 (Figure 6.4). Nevertheless, nuclear power only accounted for 1 percent of China's total installed electricity generation capacity and 1.9 percent of total electricity generated in 2009, which is significantly lower than that of many other countries including most industrialized nations and some major emerging markets (Table 6.3). As of July 2011, China's installed nuclear power capacity ranked only the ninth in the world (Figure 6.4).

Amidst growing consciousness about climate change and energy shortage, the Chinese government, which perceives nuclear energy as a clean, efficient, and safe alternative to conventional fossil fuels, has made up its mind to speed up the construction of nuclear reactors in the near future, including some of the world's most advanced, with targeted installed capacity reaching at least 80 GW by 2020, 200 GW by 2030, and 400 GW by 2050 (World Nuclear Association 2011a). As

Table 6.3 Nuclear power's share of electricity production in 13 countries, 2009

Country	*Nuclear share of electricity production (%)*
France	75.2
Ukraine	48.6
Hungary	43.0
South Korea	34.8
Japan	28.9
Germany	26.1
USA	20.2
UK	17.9
Russia	17.8
Canada	14.8
Brazil	3.0
India	2.2
China	1.9

Source: World Nuclear Association.

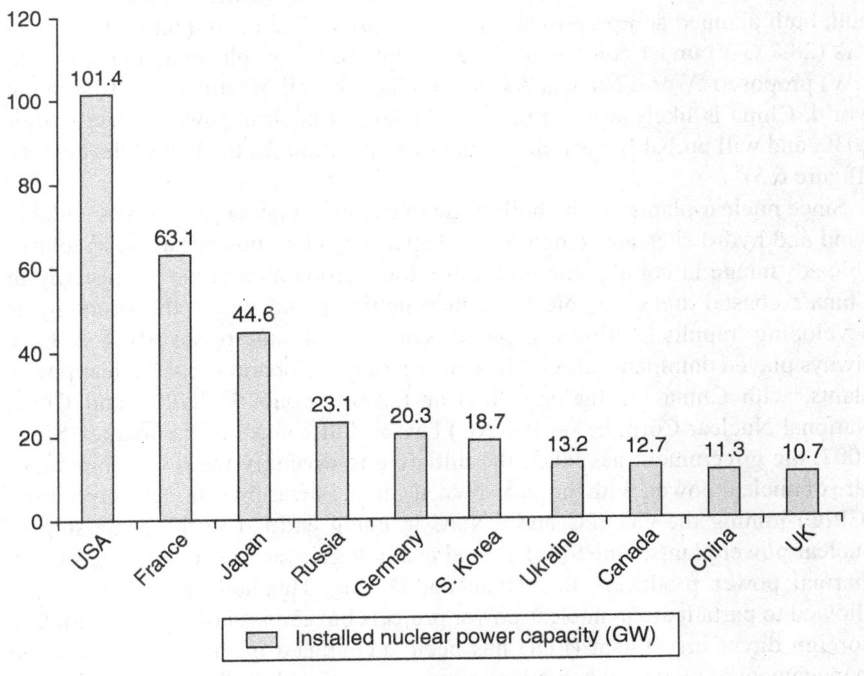

Figure 6.4 Top ten countries by installed nuclear power capacity.

Source: World Nuclear Association (2011b).

the country is rapidly becoming self-sufficient in reactor design and construction, as well as other aspects of the fuel cycle, it has revised its energy industry strategy from "moderately develop nuclear power" in the 10th Five-Year Plan (2001–05) to "actively develop nuclear power" in the 11th Five-Year Plan (2006–10). Nuclear power was also underlined in a five trillion yuan (US$0.78 trillion) alternative energy plan between 2011 and 2020 drafted by the National Energy Administration. According to the revised plan that supports a Great Leap Forward in nuclear development, the Chinese government has reset its 2020 target of installed nuclear power capacity at 86 GW, more than doubled from the earlier target of 40 GW in the "Nuclear Power Medium- and Long-Term Development Plan (2005–20)" drafted by the National Development and Reform Commission in 2007 (*China Daily Online* 2009b). If the revised 2020 target is fulfilled, China's installed nuclear power capacity is expected to see a ninefold increase from the 9 GW capacity it had achieved by the end of 2009. Accordingly, the 2020 targeted share of nuclear power in total installed capacity has also been revised up from 4 percent to 5 percent. In order to achieve the goal, the government will not only emphasize nuclear power development in coastal provinces as before, but also try to establish a number of nuclear power plants in inland provinces like Jiangxi, Anhui, Hunan, Hubei, Jilin, Henan, Sichuan, and Gansu. The geographic shift of nuclear power development is in accord with China's long-term strategy of moving economic centers from coastal areas to western hinterlands.

China today has the world's largest nuclear power capacity under construction, both planned and proposed. As of July 2011, China had a total of 26 reactors (28.7 GW) under construction, 52 reactors (60 GW) planned, and 120 (123 GW) proposed (World Nuclear Association 2011b), all of which rank first in the world. China is likely to have the world's largest nuclear power capacity after 2030, and will probably keep the number one position for the rest of the century (Figure 6.5).

Since nuclear plants can be built close to centers of demand, whereas suitable wind and hydro sites are remote from demand, nuclear power has an irreplaceable advantage in comparison with other low-carbon alternatives, especially in China's coastal areas, remote from the coalfields and where the economy is developing rapidly. China's gigantic state-owned enterprises (SOEs) have always played dominant roles in the construction and operation of nuclear power plants, with China Guangdong Nuclear Power Group (CGNPC) and China National Nuclear Corporation (CNNC) having full control of the market. Since 2007, the government has taken the initiative to diversify the ownership structure of nuclear power, with the state-owned China Power Investment Corporation (CPIC) joining the CGNPC and CNNC in being entitled to the ownership of nuclear power plants. Due to safety and technology concerns, other state-owned thermal power producers like Huaneng, Datang, Huadian, and Guodian are allowed to participate in nuclear power projects but cannot hold majority stakes. Foreign direct investment (FDI) has been encouraged in the construction and management of nuclear power plants on the condition that Chinese partners hold the majority of shares and foreign enterprises hold the advanced technologies.

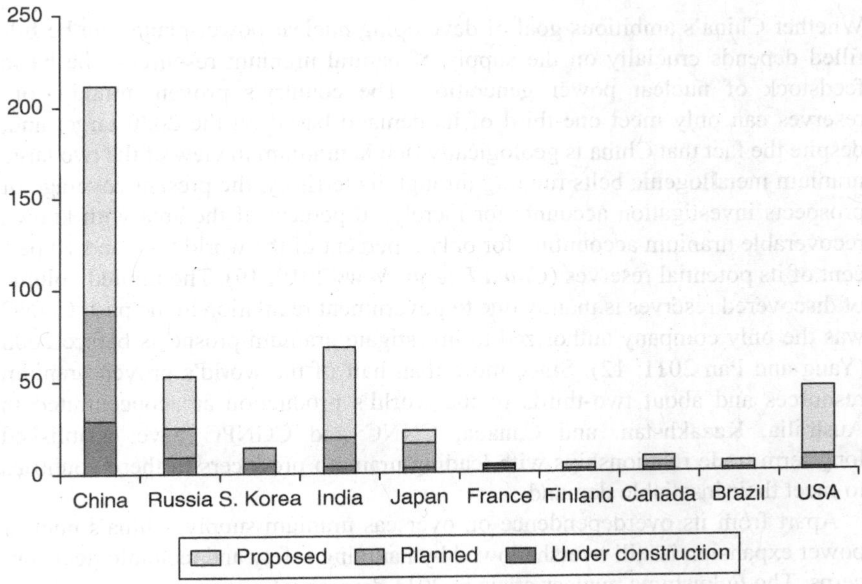

Figure 6.5 Nuclear power capacity under construction, planned, and proposed (GW).

Source: World Nuclear Association (2011b).

As for the manufacture of equipment, FDI had been encouraged in the production of nuclear power reactors of over 600 MW between 2004 and 2007, but after the Chinese Ministry of Commerce revised the "Catalogue for the Guidance of Foreign Investment Industries" in 2007, FDI has only been encouraged in the manufacture of equipment for nuclear power plants with a larger capacity of over 1 GW (Yang and Pan 2011: 5–6).

China is heavily dependent upon foreign technology in the design of nuclear power reactors, but it has been vigorously pursuing indigenous technology over which it has intellectual property rights. China's two mainstream reactor types are based on the second-generation-plus design from Areva, France, and the third-generation design from Westinghouse, a US company. In recent years, CNNC has been working on the China Experimental Fast Reactor, which is the key to fourth-generation technology. It made a breakthrough in successfully testing the first China Experimental Fast Reactor in July 2010, making China the eighth country in the world to own the technology (*Xinhua News* 2010). Compared with the third-generation reactors which have a utility rate of uranium of just one percent, the China Experimental Fast Reactor greatly reduces the consumption of uranium and boasts a utility rate of more than 60 percent. The technological breakthrough in the fourth-generation reactor may, in the long run, help China to cope with the scarcity of natural uranium resources for nuclear power development.

Challenges in nuclear power development

Whether China's ambitious goal of developing nuclear power plants can be fulfilled depends crucially on the supply of natural uranium resources, the basic feedstock of nuclear power generation. The country's proven uranium ore reserves can only meet one-third of its demand based on the 2020 target and, despite the fact that China is geologically rich in uranium in view of the two large uranium metallogenic belts running through its territory, the present coverage of prospects investigation accounts for merely 50 percent of the area with known recoverable uranium accounting for only 3 percent of the world total and 10 percent of its potential reserves (*China Energy News* 2010: 19). The limited volume of discovered reserves is mainly due to government regulation in the past: CNNC was the only company authorized to investigate uranium prospects before 2008 (Yang and Pan 2011: 12). Since more than half of the world's proven uranium resources and about two-thirds of the world's production are concentrated in Australia, Kazakhstan, and Canada, CNNC and CGNPC have established long-term trade relationships with leading uranium producers in these countries to meet their insatiable demand.

Apart from its overdependence on overseas uranium supply, China's nuclear power expansion is still overshadowed by haunting safety and technological concerns. The Fukushima nuclear crisis in 2011 dramatically prompted a worldwide review of the safety of nuclear power projects, which had thrived previously in many parts of the world due to climate change and energy shortage concerns. Public objection again becomes a major obstacle to the construction of local nuclear power projects, while the safe treatment of nuclear waste containing radioactive materials poses another challenge.

7 Tianjin: model city of low-carbon economy

For a vast continental state like China, it is an essential step in the national fight against climate change to establish low-carbon provinces, regions, and large-scale cities for various piloting programs since local mitigation efforts can be more effectively managed based on regional industry make-up and local climate and socioeconomic factors and, therefore, be the necessary predecessor to nationwide action. Places like California (the United States), Vancouver (Canada), Vaxjo (Sweden), and Masdar City, Abu Dhabi (United Arab Emirates) have taken the lead in formulating aggressive low-carbon or even carbon-neutral plans that support sustainable economic development and a green lifestyle. No nation, however, has been setting up low-carbon regions or cities on the scale that China is currently undertaking, where massive urbanization and industrialization have precipitated enormous opportunities to create green economic clusters and stimulated serious environmental risks linked with increasing production and consumption simultaneously. The Chinese government announced its low-carbon pilot provinces and cities program in 2010, which covered five provinces, including Guangdong, Liaoning, Hubei, Shaanxi, and Yunnan and eight cities, including Tianjin, Chongqing, Shenzhen, Xiamen, Nanchang, Guiyang, Baoding, and Hangzhou (*People's Daily Online* 2010a). According to the National Development and Reform Commission that launched the program, the experimental areas should include the work on climate change in the local five-year plans and establish operational goals, major tasks, and specific measures of controlling local emissions of greenhouse gases. Among the eight pilot cities, Tianjin has been placed first in the pecking order, which usually implies prioritized importance in China's political context. Tianjin, as a low-carbon model city, also attracted international attention when Japan's trade minister, Masayuki Naoshima said, in an APEC ministerial meeting in June 2010, that Tianjin may be chosen as APEC's first low-carbon city to test new technology including smart grids and renewable-power generation as part of efforts to reduce dependence on fossil fuels (*Bloomberg News* 2010). Actually, Tianjin's low-carbon effort had begun long before it was officially chosen as a model city for pioneering climate and energy programs, with past experiences having demonstrated that designated low-carbon cities and regions can help to create a friendly environment for the creation and deployment of low-carbon technologies in buildings, transport, infrastructure, energy utilization, and industrial production, which represent leading economic opportunities and replicable models of sustainable development.

It seems to be a mission impossible for a booming manufacturing powerhouse with double digit GDP growth to lead the low-carbon and circular economy but, according to the Tianjin Municipal Master Plan (2005–20), one of Tianjin's strategic goals is to build itself into a liveable city with a good ecological environment (Tianjin Municipal Government 2007). Orientated as China's third growth pole, paralleled with Shanghai and Shenzhen, Tianjin differs from its peers in its special focus on environmental protection and energy conservation. Such green commitment is closely related to China's new-century ambition of improving energy efficiency and restructuring its economy in a low-carbon direction. In the 1980s, Shenzhen was chosen by the central government as a major special economic zone to duplicate the adjacent successful development model of Hong Kong, while Shanghai, with its Pudong New District in particular, became the symbol of China's further economic liberalization characterized by financial reform and continued opening-up in the 1990s. After more than two decades of high-speed economic growth, China has realized that mounting environmental problems like water and air pollution, desertification, and loss of biodiversity have become so severe that they not only threaten the sustainable development of the economy, people's health, and ordinary life, but also pose an acute political challenge to the governance of the ruling Communist Party. When the Chinese government was trying to designate Tianjin as the next experimental zone for further economic restructuring in northern China, energy-saving and environmental issues, once ignored by Shanghai and Shenzhen planners, naturally became new policy focuses in the reconstruction of this port city that had for a long time been overshadowed by the capital city of Beijing. Climate-related low-carbon effort is not only an image issue for China, but also a good opportunity to address the country's serious energy shortage problem caused by growing demand, inefficient use, and limited energy reserves. The relationship between economic growth and energy utilization matters greatly, not only from an emissions perspective, but from an energy security perspective as well. In the context of sustainable development, it is no wonder that, as a pilot city of new-found reform and opening-up, Tianjin is expected by the central government to function, not only as a business hub and international port, but also as a model city for a low-carbon economy and environmental protection.

Tianjin's low-carbon policies

When the National Development and Reform Commission, China's top economic planners, was drafting the first development plan for energy-saving and environmental protection industries in the 12th Five-Year Plan period (2011–15), Tianjin's Development and Reform Commission, together with the College of Environmental Science and Engineering of the Nankai University and Tianjin University of Technology, was working on Tianjin's own Five-Year Plan for a low-carbon economy. Planners have agreed to speed up the development of the industrial, communication and construction sectors involved with low-carbon emissions, to develop the low-emission service industry and renewable energy and to push forward low-carbon consumption. Tianjin's Binhai New Area has decided to invest 14 billion yuan (US$2.2 billion) in 2011 and 2012 to build the low-carbon industrial cluster and develop renewable energy (sina.com news 2010). The Binhai New Area is all set to ban energy-guzzling and heavily polluted enterprises from being located in the New Area, and has asked local administrative regions to distribute emission-cutting targets to individual companies and projects. Now the Binhai New Area is devoted to the construction of Tianjin Economic-Technological Development Area (TEDA) and Dagang District as an ecological industrial park, as well as the development of solar energy, methane, and geothermal energy.

TEDA is among the first to obtain the identity of a national-level pilot zone for circular economy. As part of the new energy industry receiving priority support, the wind energy sector covering turbines, key component parts, R&D, and services receives incentives from the central government, Tianjin Municipality, and TEDA. Domestic and international heavyweight wind turbine makers like Vestas, Gamesa, and Suzlon are clustering in Tianjin, which is becoming a production base for wind energy equipment. Major preferential policies announced by TEDA to attract wind energy-related enterprises are as follows:

- Land rent subsidy shall be provided for a wind energy equipment producer newly incorporated in TEDA for purchasing land for production within TEDA, in accordance with the scale and density of its investment and its project quality.
- Rent subsidies shall be provided for different categories of wind energy equipment producers newly incorporated in TEDA for the lease of standard factory buildings within TEDA. (The maximum subsidy will be 15 yuan/m^2 per month). Such a producer shall enjoy a full subsidy in accordance with the standard agreed on between the producer and the TEDA competent authority for one year since the date of the lease and a 50 percent subsidy in the following two years. The maximal subsidized area of leased standard factory buildings is 4,000 m^2.
- A technology-intensive wind energy equipment producer, upon the appraisal of the TEDA competent authority, shall enjoy a subsidy of a maximum of 50 percent of the annual interest rate (calculated at the benchmark interest rate) of their loan for investment in fixed assets. However, the subsidy shall not exceed 50 percent of the recipient's contribution to the disposable revenue of TEDA of the same year. The maximal time limit for enjoying the interest subsidy shall be three years and the accumulative maximum shall be three million yuan.
- Financial support of 500,000 yuan to one million yuan shall be granted to a non-independent R&D institution (affiliated to various production-oriented businesses) engaging in the development of a product or technology falling

into the encouraged hi-tech sectors receiving TEDA's priority support. Financial support of five million yuan at the maximum shall be provided for a foreign-funded R&D institution with an independent legal entity, whose investment shall be at least US$5 million and who engages in the product and technological R&D in a hi-tech sector receiving priority support of TEDA.

- A financial reward equal to 5 percent of the transaction value of an independent hi-tech achievement transfer within TEDA by an R&D organization with independent legal entity shall be granted after the successful commercialization of the achievement. The maximum amount of the financial reward shall be one million yuan. However, such a reward shall not be granted to technological transfer between related organizations.
- A financial reward equal to 80 percent of the annual individual income tax paid to the local government of TEDA shall be granted within a period of five years to a top-notch talent, highly skilled HR technician earning an annual salary of above 50,000 yuan and managerial staff earning annual salaries of above 80,000 yuan.
- TEDA shall provide senior managerial staff and technological staff apartments or housing subsidy for two years.
- TEDA encourages businesses and R&D organizations to set up postdoctoral stations or postdoctoral innovation and practice bases. Financial support of 50,000 yuan shall be granted for the R&D work of a postdoctoral station and 30,000 yuan for a postdoctoral innovation and practice base.

(TEDA Investment Promotion Bureau 2010)

Since the Kyoto Protocol took effect in 2005, TEDA has been encouraging local enterprises to apply for the Clean Development Mechanism (CDM) projects that need approval from the United Nations and sell carbon credits to international buyers. It is estimated that environmental projects in TEDA are now selling emission reductions totaling more than 500,000 tons of CO_2 equivalent every year under the UN carbon trading system (*Tianjin Daily* 2009: 11). In October 2008, China's first national emission trading marketplace, the Tianjin Emissions Exchange, was unveiled in the Financial Street of TEDA. Chicago Climate Exchange, the world's first global marketplace for integrating voluntary legally binding emissions reductions with emissions trading and offsets for all six greenhouse gases, provides technology and system support for the Exchange, and owns 25 percent of the shares. The other two equity participants are CNPC Assets Management (53 percent) and Tianjin Property Rights Exchange (22 percent) (CNPC Press Release 2008). Like the Beijing and Shanghai exchanges, the Tianjin Emissions Exchange does not cover the trading of CO_2 since the relevant government departments are still examining that issue. For now. the Exchange mainly focuses on the trading of major pollutant credits such as SO_2 and COD (chemical oxygen demand).

In 2010, TEDA won the opportunity to start the EU Switch-Asia TBNA (Tianjin Binhai New Area) Industrial Symbiosis Project, which was financed by the European Union and United Nations Industrial Development Organization (UNIDO)

(*China Daily Online* 2010). The four-year Switch-Asia project in TEDA required 1.85 million euros of investment, of which the EU contributed 1.48 million euros. Industrial symbiosis is a novel approach to ensuring environmentally sustainable industrial development, such as by establishing an energy-efficient supply chain system. The TEDA Low Carbon Promotion Center, its supplementary project, is expected to serve as an information- and technology-sharing platform for carbon emission reduction and energy efficiency enhancement. Tianjin is also planning soon to impose a mandatory limit on energy used to heat buildings, probably the first city-wide carbon cap-and-trade system in China. Property managers able to reduce energy use to below the limit will earn credits which they can then sell.

Progress in reducing energy consumption and developing a low-carbon economy

In 2009, Tianjin's energy intensity, referring to energy consumption per unit of GDP that is usually positively correlated to the variation of carbon emissions per unit of GDP, dropped by 6.03 percent year on year, outperforming the average decrease of 3.61 percent for the whole nation in the same year (Tianjin Environmental Protection Bureau 2010). In 2009, two major pollutants in Tianjin, SO_2 and COD, both dropped by 1 percent year on year, slower than their previous decline rates in 2008 (1.9 percent and 3.03 percent respectively). By the end of 2009, the newly built greenbelt area in Tianjin was about 28 million m^2. In 2009, for 84.1 percent of the total days (307 days) Tianjin's urban air quality was equal to or better than the Grade II standard set by the Ministry of Environment (Air Pollution Index ≤ 100), a little lower than its rate of 88 percent in 2008 (Tianjin Environmental Protection Bureau 2010). For eight consecutive years, the quality of all drinking water sources in Tianjin has reached the national standard.

Wind farm projects

Tianjin Dashentang Wind Farm, the first wind farm under construction in Tianjin, started equipment installation in February 2010. It lies south of Sajintuo Village of Hangu of Binhai New Area and is 4 km from the east of Dashentang village. Its installed capacity is 26 MW and the investment in it totals 370 million yuan. The wind farm will install wind turbines with independent intellectual property rights whose unit capacity is the largest for commercial operation on land, whose blade diameter is the longest, and whose technology is the most advanced at present. In addition, it will adopt, for the first time, the world's most advanced distributed grid access method. The wind farm will provide clean and reliable green power of 52,130,000 kilowatt-hours (kWh) each year for the development and construction of Binhai New Area and will provide power for over 50,000 households on the basis that each household consumes 87 kWh of power each month. Each year, the wind farm is expected to save the country typical consumption of 19,000 tons of coal, 30,400 tons of water, and to reduce emission of 6,000 tons of CO_2, 88 tons of nitrogen oxide, 10.4 tons of smoke dust, and 39.2 tons of sulfur dioxide.

Electric car and battery projects

China, with the largest automobile market in the world, has announced policies to wean consumers off fossil-fuelled vehicles by offering substantial purchase subsidies for green cars and financing for the construction of electric power charging infrastructure. In May 2010, Premier Wen Jiabao visited Tianjin Lishen Battery Co. Ltd, a leading enterprise in China for the development of green Li-ion batteries. Meanwhile, US Secretary of Commerce Gary Locke also visited the battery manufacturing facility in Tianjin operated by Lio Energy Systems, a joint venture between Lishen Power Battery and CODA, a California-based battery system and electric car company. In July 2009, China National Offshore Oil Corporation (CNOOC) signed an agreement with Tianjin Jinneng Investment Company to start the reorganization of Tianjin Lishen. Following the reorganization, Tianjin Lishen has planned to invest 5 billion yuan on battery production lines for 200,000 electric cars (CNOOC press release 2010).

Clean coal projects

The Asian Development Bank (ADB) approved a US$135 million loan to help China build a 250-megawatt coal-fired integrated gasification combined cycle (IGCC) plant in Tianjin City that can generate up to 1,470 gigawatt-hours of electricity every year (*People's Daily Online* 2010b). To reduce greenhouse gas emissions and acid rain, China has launched a clean coal power generation program, GreenGen, with the Tianjin project being the cornerstone of the first phase. ADB will also provide US$1.25 million in technical assistance for the second and third phases of the program, which will result in a scaled-up IGCC plant fitted with carbon capture and storage technology by 2013. As the IGCC technology reduces greenhouse gas emissions, the project is expected to be capable of producing certified emission reductions (CERs) under the Clean Development Mechanism (CDM) of the Kyoto Protocol. ADB is providing technical support for the CDM application process. ADB said that it is providing a US$5 million grant from its Climate Change Fund to finance direct supervision and technical support from the component suppliers during the critical initial operation and maintenance phase. China Huaneng Group is the executing agency for the Tianjin IGCC project.

Solar cell projects

The United Solar Ovonic (Uni-Solar), a US subsidiary of Energy Conversion Devices, and Tianjin Jinneng Investment Company, set up a joint venture in Tianjin to convert US-made solar cells into solar modules for the Chinese market. United Solar undertakes about 75 percent of the manufacturing in Michigan and then ships it to Tianjin, where the joint venture company completes the process and cuts the finished product up into the proper sizes (*Reuters News* 2010). In May 2010, US Secretary of Commerce Gary Locke paid a visit to the joint venture in Tianjin. Uni-Solar signed an agreement during Locke's trip to sell

500 kilowatts of its thin-film solar laminates to NYKE Solar Integrators, a Chinese company, for a demonstration project (*Reuters News* 2010).

Low-carbon projects in China-Singapore Tianjin Eco-city

On 1 December 2009, Sino-Singapore Tianjin Investment and Development Company (SSTEC), master-developer of the China-Singapore Tianjin Eco-city (a bilateral cooperative project between the Chinese and Singaporean governments), penned a memorandum of understanding (MOU) with Samsung C&T Corporation to create the first-of-its-kind green central business district (CBD), also known as the Eco-CBD, in the China-Singapore Tianjin Eco-city. This Eco-CBD aims to integrate economic, social, and community activities in a sustainable manner and demonstrate that environmental conservation and urbanization can progress in tandem with economic activities.

On 30 December 2009, the SSTEC started to develop a 130-hectare Eco-Industrial Park (EIP) in the China-Singapore Tianjin Eco-city. Positioned as a premier eco manufacturing base for eco investors in the Bohai Rim area, the EIP will be home to light clean industries from green business clusters, including clean energy, green building, green transport, clean water, clean waste management, and clean environment. Estimated to cost 4 billion yuan to develop, the park is expected to generate 10,000 jobs when completed.

In May 2010, the SSTEC signed three industrial land deals involving more than 1 billion yuan in investments in the Eco Business Park (EBP) and the EIP. In addition, SSTEC also announced strategic collaborations with three companies in the green technology field. Tianjin House Construction Development Group Co. Ltd announced an investment of 300 million yuan to develop low-carbon and energy-efficient green buildings in the EBP. Keppel DHCS Pte Ltd (KDHCS) has plans to develop and operate a district heating and cooling system in the EBP. SSTEC signed an MOU with the Hitachi Group as strategic technology partner for test-bedding and development of eco solutions in the areas of Home Energy Management Systems (HEMS) and Electric Vehicle (EV) Charging solutions, Building Energy Management Systems (BEMS), Community Energy Management Systems (CEMS), smart grid, and water management solutions. SSTEC also formed a strategic partnership with Singapore Technologies Electronics Limited (ST Electronics) for the development of green solutions for intelligent building management and energy saving systems, intelligent transport management systems, eLearning solutions and training, and simulation systems for the Eco-City (SSTEC 2010).

China-Singapore Tianjin Eco-city Project: norms and functions

The galloping rate of progress of industrialization and urbanization in China has brought about mounting environmental and social problems, including water and energy shortage, air pollution, overcrowding, traffic congestion, loss of biodiversity, and desertification. Influenced by the internationally popular concept of "eco-city" that focuses on integrating sustainability into city planning, the Chinese government, in recent years, has been paying increasing attention to the know-how involved in building cities in balance with nature. As the notions of "eco-city" and "garden city" are imported, and China is still in the take-off stage of economic development, the country has been enthusiastic about cooperating with other foreign partners in eco-city projects in the past few years, with the flagship China-Singapore Tianjin Eco-city Project being the best known and most successful to date. Based on its indigenous experience with the construction of "ecological garden cities" (*shengtai yuanlin chengshi*), China has also made efforts to plan and build its own eco-cities in some localities. China's Ministry of Housing and Urban-Rural Development has standardized the assessment indexes to measure "ecological garden cities," with a string of environmentally friendly cities like Qingdao, Yangzhou, Nanjing, Hangzhou, Weihai, Suzhou, and Guilin already on the list. The per capita green land in an "ecological garden city" must reach at least 12 m^2 with greenery coverage of over 45 percent and more than 300 "blue sky" days in a year. A "blue sky" day is when the Air Pollution Index (API) is equal to, or lower than, 100, which means the pollutant concentrations of SO_2, NO_2, PM10, CO and O_3 in the atmosphere should not exceed 0.15, 0.12, 0.15, 10 and 0.2 mg/m^3 respectively.

The trajectory of the Singapore-China project-based cooperation from the Suzhou Industrial Park (1994) to the Tianjin Eco-city (2008) has manifested China's shift in its economic strategy from building itself into an export-oriented manufacturing base to a service-driven and low-carbon economy. Compared with the unilateral nature of the knowledge transfer from Singapore to China in the Suzhou Industrial Park project, the Singaporean side has found its participation in the Eco-city project to a larger extent an expertise-sharing and mutual-learning interaction between the two countries, since pollution and energy problems have pushed the rising China to lead the world in tapping renewable energy. At the strategic level, it marks Singapore's continued efforts to stay relevant to China's rise by identifying a niche area for collaboration with China. In doing so, Singapore can leverage on China's growth. On China's part, the project enables the country to devise a model that balances the goals of economic growth, environment protection, and social harmony, one that is based on Singapore's own developmental experience, which may be more realistic and attractive to China when compared to other models. This is in line with the top leadership's call for a scientific concept of development enshrined in the constitution of the Chinese Communist Party. The project will also facilitate the implementation of China's regional development strategies (Singapore's Ministry of National Development press release 2008a).

Considering the increasing importance of today's cities and urban construction in determining the carbon intensity and levels of pollutant affecting our modern life, building cities in a more environmentally friendly and sustainable way has become a possible solution to demanding environmental problems faced by the international community. The relatively new concept of "eco-city" has been envisioned and put into practice by avant-garde architects and urban planners in order to create the smallest possible ecological footprint for city dwellers. The city exists, like everything else, in an evolving universe, but it appears to have a special role in evolution that may have a great deal to do with how we build and use it (Register 2002: 38). A successful city must balance economic, social, and ecological needs on all sides. The notion of "eco-city" or ecopolis is a big step forward in the long-term evolution of human urban construction. Such a city minimizes the required consumption of energy, water, and raw materials and its waste discharge of air, solid, and water pollutants. The year 2007 marked a watershed in human history when, for the first time, half of the world's population was living in cities (UNEP *et al.* 2007: 1). As hubs of prosperity, cities have also been blamed for causing environmental degradation due to the high-carbon lifestyle and huge amount of waste output they encompass. It is therefore, extremely important to understand that one of the most effective solutions to current environmental problems on a global scale lies in the way we plan and build our cities.

No single recipe for urban sustainability can be applied to all cities, but the various "eco-city" schemes should share the three common goals of conservation, recycling, and preservation of biodiversity. Designers of these cities should always bear in mind that economic, social, and environmental considerations are always interconnected, and that current urban development should not compromise the ability of future generations to meet their own needs. It is important for "eco-city" planners to manage environmental resources as strategic assets that are essential to the long-term interest of urban residents. Environmental resources such as clean air, fresh water, forest and open space are often taken for granted by city planners who do not pay enough attention to their efficient and sustainable utilization. In an "eco-city," clean air and drinking water sources that are crucial to human health should not be polluted in exchange for economic development. Biodiversity within and nearby the city should be protected for the sake of the balance of nature and the resilience of ecosystems to environmental change. Forests should be preserved, not only because they are necessary watersheds and habitats, but also because they absorb a huge amount of greenhouse gases and thus slow down the global warming trend. More trees should be planted in the city area or the suburbs to purify the atmosphere and avoid the formation of urban heat islands (UHIs), metropolitan areas which are significantly warmer than their surrounding rural areas. Other important environmental resources such as wetlands, coral reefs, and mangroves should also be preserved in the process of urban expansion.

A typical eco-city, underlining the urgency of the global climate change issue, should be a low-carbon city with improved public transport and an increase in pedestrianization and cycling to reduce car emissions. To minimize the use of automobiles, the city should be compact and different from the general urban pattern today (i.e. skyscrapers in the middle with tens of thousands of acres of ground-scrapers sprawling all around). Instead, the blueprint should be a multi-center one and in each center or subcenter, catering, education, medical care, and shopping services should be available to most residents.

Dense subcenters and compact neighborhood centers are situated fairly close to the major city hub. High-rise buildings are still encouraged in center areas to save land and thus reduce the number of long-distance commuters that may have to depend on cars. Some of the outlying communities will be agricultural villages providing their own farm produce for the city hub and subcenters.

High population density, therefore, is a necessity for a sustainable city because it not only reduces the per capita demand for occupied land, but also cuts per capita cost of supplying piped water, sewer systems, refuse collection, postal delivery, and other public services. An eco-city must provide easy access to daily necessities and entertainment by walking, cycling, and public transportation. A new transportation hierarchy should be established prioritizing pedestrians, cyclists, subways, buses and, finally, private automobiles. Roads may be narrow to make walking easy and driving difficult.

New energy-saving building materials should be widely used in the construction of an eco-city. To achieve low emissions, architects sometimes need to fit the buildings with solar panels to produce electricity, which will be used for lighting, office equipment, and air conditioning. Better ventilation strategies should be worked out for reducing dependence upon air conditioning. Blinds, the opacity of windows, and airflow must be regulated throughout the building to conserve energy for heating and for balanced natural lighting. The eco-city should make use of water resources conservatively and interfere minimally with the intrinsic patterns of the water cycle in the ecological system. A compact city layout is necessary to reduce the footprint on permeable soil, and efficient water recycling systems making full use of watercourses and reservoirs should be established to regulate run-offs in both the rainy and dry seasons and convert rainwater into useful and drinkable fresh water. Urban aquifers should be strictly protected from overuse or pollution, while the soil's permeability should be guaranteed to ensure the absorption of groundwater.

An eco-city should be a "garden city" surrounded by greenbelts and woodlands, promoting the preservation of local species and harmonious coexistence between humans and other creatures. Biodiversity increases the resilience of ecosystems to environmental changes. Rivers, lakes, wetland, and forest resources can be used as protected areas to add to urban biodiversity in the way the city is built. If urban waste is carefully limited and recycled, and local people take full responsibility for ensuring that their daily activities do not threaten the existence of other species, the city itself can become a botanical garden where urbanism does not lead to a confrontation between humanity and other animals and plants. An eco-city also includes arcologies that take less land, less energy to operate and require less connecting materials such as pipes and wires. In an arcological city, major social, economic, and civic activities are available within short distances, and farm production is located just outside the city gates. Individual buildings, communities, and the city as a whole should be maintained with great efficiency and little waste.

In order to achieve urban development projects with integrated sustainable solutions across all sectors, eco-city guidelines and objectives have to be interwoven with local requirements (Gaffron *et al.* 2008: 37). Confronted with the complexity that characterizes the real processes of the construction of the city today, urban planners need to promote cooperation in a multidisciplinary planning team as well as among all stakeholders. An eco-city should be understood as a single integrated system (holistic approach) and not as a combination or result of many sectoral developments planned in isolation (Gaffron *et al.* 2008: 18). The idea of integrated planning is the basis for sustainable urbanism, demanding a repeated and ongoing process of analysis and a multidisciplinary approach to sustainability. In eco-city planning, those sectors related to the metabolic and environmental functions of the city (transport, energy and material flows, and socioeconomic aspects), which conventional planning deems subsidiary to urban structure, are considered to be at the same level of importance (Gaffron *et al.* 2008: 37–38). Extensive participation is an important part of knowledge-based eco-city planning because the more the stakeholders are involved in decision-making, the more knowledge they will contribute to the bottom-up planning process. As grass-root democracy has been regarded as an indispensable element for good environmental governance, public participation should be an iterative process throughout the planning process.

With the active participation of different sectors and relevant stakeholders, the whole process of eco-city planning and construction is usually focused on such key areas as urban structure, transportation, energy, and other resource efficiency, as well as the socioeconomic aspect. The main principles for sustainable urban development (i.e. minimizing the use of land, energy, and materials and minimizing the impairment of natural environment) should always be followed throughout the construction process.

Urban structure

The efficient use of land resource is a basic requirement for eco-city planning. Eco-city planners have to pay sufficient attention to the spatial level of quarters and neighborhoods. It is necessary to optimize the density of settlements with regard to the potentially contradictory requirements of transportation (higher density of origins and destinations), solar architecture (depending on the climate: either avoiding shading between buildings or using it for passive cooling) and quality of life issues (such as open spaces for climatic and social functions and personal comfort) (Gaffron *et al.* 2008: 25). Instead of detached, single-family houses with large gardens, compact building structures, such as multi-storey residential, commercial, or mixed-use buildings, should be considered. Habitats for plants and animals must be created or conserved in urban contexts, with sufficient open space and green areas maintained in the form of gardens, parks, street-trees, green roofs, green facades, and natural water features.

Transportation

There is no doubt that eco-city planning should make public transport a top priority when addressing air pollution and climate change issues. A variety of tools that involve policies on car parking, car access, and car ownership should be used to reduce travel by private car. Economic tools, including road tolls for lorries and private cars as well as subsidies for rail transport, can be adopted to encourage people to choose low-carbon transport. Eco-city designers should give first preference to an arrangement that reduces the need for transport, then to those measures that encourage travel at low speed, third to public transport and mass transit, and finally to limited use of car transport. The compact and multi-centric layout of an eco-city should allow most travel to take place on foot, by bike, and by public transport. Only a small proportion of the population drive private cars, with special taxes in place to encourage them to buy hybrid vehicles that use energy more efficiently. Yet urban planners should bear in mind that alternatives must be of maximum quality when reducing accessibility for the car. Otherwise the transport inconvenience will provoke public dissatisfaction or even sharp criticism.

Energy and resource efficiency

Determining how to use energy and other resources efficiently and sustainably is the key part of an eco-city project. Measures should be taken to minimize the energy demand of the built urban structure and minimize the energy loss of buildings. The use of fossil fuel for air-conditioning and other electricity supply should be limited, while a variety of renewable energies are to be used widely. Urban architects should design more solar architecture in the city to make better use of clean energy from the sun, giving preference to environmentally friendly and sustainably produced materials. Advanced devices should be adopted to treat wastewater so that it can be recirculated into the water cycle without negative impacts, and the collection and purification of rainwater will help city dwellers to use natural resources more efficiently. Solid waste should be recycled or reused, with special devices introduced to use landfill gases as a form of new energy and thus reduce greenhouse gas emissions.

Social infrastructure and economic viability

Besides environmental protection, the eco-city as an attractive and prosperous place has to provide a satisfying social and economic infrastructure for high-quality life. One important element is easy access to day-to-day facilities. Kindergarten and elementary schools should be located within walking distance, while other schools, clinics, and hospitals should be within walking/cycling distance or a maximum of 30 minutes by public transport. Leisure and recreation facilities, such as cinemas, theatres, and fitness centers should also be within walking distance or easily reached by public transport.

To launch an eco-city with comparatively high construction costs and make it sustainable, economic viability is another important aspect worthy of attention from the outset. To achieve economic sustainability it is generally helpful to involve a plurality of investors, including owner-inhabitants, real-estate companies, and professional developers right from the start. A public-private partnership (PPP) is one of the tools available for implementing eco-cities, with different partners from the public and the private sectors working together. Cooperation of all sectors on eco-city projects makes it possible to divide the risks among partners, to attain the public, social, and societal goals with reduced funding from public sources, and to raise the return on investment on related private investments. Short-term investments and returns should not be the only index for measuring the profitability of an eco-city project, whose long-term success relies on whether it helps to create a unique city context with significant reduction of pollution, minimized use of fossil fuel and other resources, improvement of people's health, high quality of life, fewer car accidents, and greater convenience for social activities.

Monitoring and evaluation

When the physical construction is completed, it is time to evaluate the real performances of the eco-city and test whether the planning hypotheses are validated. Certain monitoring and evaluation mechanisms and procedures must be in place to ensure that the urban development process serves the goals of conserving resources, reducing pollution, increasing green spaces, and improving people's residential life. Such evaluation is also important for acquiring valuable empirical knowledge that can be used as reference information for future improvement and other eco-cities' design. One indispensable feature of the eco-city is public participation, so a good monitoring system not only depends on the technical methods of data collecting on energy saving, emission reduction, and water consumption, but also depends on well-designed social feedback mechanisms that assimilate public opinions and assessments. Continuous evaluation with the participation of all relevant stakeholders is essential for maintaining the vitality of the eco-city, which will rely on qualitative and quantitative tools to assess whether the proposed environmental, economic, and social objectives have been met. A set of indicators associated with urban structure, transport, energy, material flows, and socio-economy have to be developed to monitor urban maintenance and management. Appropriate adaptations and adjustments must be made from time to time in response to the results of the most recent evaluation.

Singapore-China cooperation in Tianjin Eco-city

The China-Singapore Tianjin Eco-City was mooted by Senior Minister Goh Chok Tong and agreed to in principle by Premier Wen Jiabao when they met in Beijing in April 2007 (*The Straits Times* 2007). The project was regarded as mutually beneficial, since Singapore and China could jointly share their experience and expertise and achieve a model for the purposes of demonstration that went beyond the confines of the project itself. Both sides have moved briskly to implement the idea.

The distinctive features of the China-Singapore Tianjin Eco-city can be viewed from two levels. The first, at the broad strategic level, will examine the framework of cooperation that oversees the implementation of this project. This framework is lacking in most other eco-city projects. The second, at the operational level, will highlight the features directly related to the project. These features may be common to other eco-city projects, although the extent of these features and the targets set may differ. The focus on the key features is not meant to suggest that this project is either bound to succeed or not succeed. Rather, the focus on the key features is intended to highlight some of the major differences between this project and other projects elsewhere.

Framework of cooperation

The China-Singapore Tianjin Eco-city project is not an ordinary commercial undertaking. In most other eco-city projects, the government's involvement is either minimal or even nonexistent. The usual practice is to let the private sector take the lead on the project with the government's role being to create the right conditions for the project to succeed. In contrast, on the China-Singapore Tianjin Eco-city project, the Singapore and Chinese governments have not only attempted to create the right conditions for the project to take off but also brought it under an official supervisory mechanism. In fact, the project has been set within the framework of bilateral cooperation between the two countries. In this sense, both governments regard the project's development as indicative of the substantive relations between the two countries. If the project progresses well, this would strengthen bilateral ties. If it does not, this might well have some negative impact on bilateral relations. It is reasonable to assert that neither the Chinese nor Singaporean governments would want to enter into such an agreement if it was not confident that the project would have a fair chance of success.

The two sides have already set up a mechanism to oversee the development of the project. The mechanism can be divided into two main levels (see Figure 7.1). The first and higher level is the Joint Steering Committee (JSC), comprising heads of the relevant ministries and government agencies from both countries and the Tianjin municipal government. Co-chaired by Deputy Prime Minister (DPM) Wong Kan Seng and Vice Premier Wang Qishan, the JSC examines all major or policy issues related to the development of the eco-city. The JSC itself reports to the Joint Council for Bilateral Cooperation (JCBC) that oversees all aspects of cooperation between Singapore and China.

Under the JSC, the relevant ministries and agencies on the Singapore side include the Ministry of National Development, Ministry of Environment and Water Resources, Ministry of Foreign Affairs, Ministry of Trade and Industry, Building and Construction Authority, International Enterprise Singapore, Jurong Town Corporation, National Parks Board, Public Utilities Board, Urban Redevelopment Authority, Housing and Development Board, and National Environment Agency. On the Chinese side, the relevant ministries and agencies include the Ministry of Housing and Urban-Rural Development, Ministry of Environmental Protection, Ministry of Land and Resources, Ministry of Foreign Affairs, and other relevant agencies.

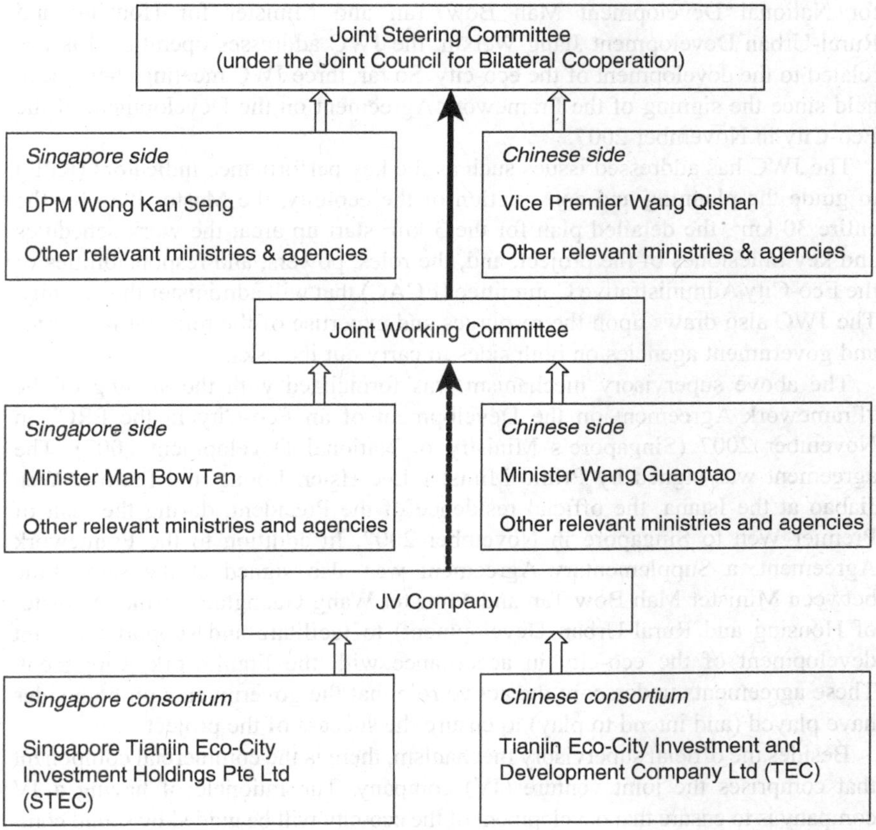

Figure 7.1 Overview of supervisory mechanism.

Source: compiled by the author.

The JSC held its inaugural meeting in Tianjin in September 2008. At that meeting, DPM Wong and Vice Premier Wang noted that the development of the eco-city had made "rapid and good progress" since the idea was mooted about one-and-a-half years ago. Most significantly, the meeting agreed that the key areas of work ahead would not only include the physical and infrastructural development of the eco-city but also cover the formulation of policies which were in line with the vision of the eco-city and the principle of the three harmonies (namely, harmony between man and man, between man and the environment, and between man and economic activities) to complement and support the project's development (Singapore's Ministry of National Development press release 2008b).

The second and lower level of the supervisory mechanism is the Joint Working Committee (JWC). The upward pointing bold arrow on Figure 7.1 indicates that the JWC reports its key deliberations directly to the JSC. Co-chaired by Minister for National Development Mah Bow Tan and Minister for Housing and Rural-Urban Development Jiang Weixin, the JWC addresses operational issues related to the development of the eco-city. So far, three JWC meetings have been held since the signing of the Framework Agreement on the Development of the Eco-City in November 2007.

The JWC has addressed issues such as the key performance indicators (KPIs) to guide the planning and construction of the eco-city, the Master Plan for the entire 30 km^2, the detailed plan for the 3 km^2 start-up area; the work schedules and key milestones of the project, and, the roles, powers, and responsibilities of the Eco-City Administrative Committee (ECAC) that will administer the eco-city. The JWC also draws upon the resources and expertise of the relevant ministries and government agencies on both sides to carry out its tasks.

The above supervisory mechanism was formalized with the signing of the "Framework Agreement on the Development of an Eco-City in the PRC" in November 2007 (Singapore's Ministry of National Development 2007). The agreement was signed by Prime Minister Lee Hsien Loong and Premier Wen Jiabao at the Istana, the official residence of the President, during the visit of Premier Wen to Singapore in November 2007. In addition to the Framework Agreement, a Supplementary Agreement was also signed at the same time between Minister Mah Bow Tan and Minister Wang Guangtao (former Minister of Housing and Rural-Urban Development) to facilitate and support the joint development of the eco-city in accordance with the Framework Agreement. These agreements underscore the active role that the governments on both sides have played (and intend to play) to ensure the success of the project.

Besides the official supervisory mechanism, there is the commercial component that comprises the joint venture (JV) company. The rationale of having a JV company is to ensure that development of the eco-city will be guided by sound commercial principles. This will ensure its financial sustainability. Operationally, the JV company exists as an independent entity. Nevertheless, the JV company indirectly reports the progress or issues that cannot be resolved at its level to the JWC which in turn reviews or addresses them. In this way, the JWC can give the project an added push when needed. This indirect relationship between the JV company and the JWC is denoted in Figure 7.1 by the upward pointing dotted arrow.

Known as the Sino-Singapore Tianjin Eco-City Investment and Development Company, the JV company has an initial registered capital of 4 billion yuan (US$583 million) with equal contributions from the Singapore consortium and the Chinese consortium. Under the JV Agreement signed on 1 July 2008, the Chinese consortium will transfer land for the development of the eco-city to the JV company as its contribution in kind to the registered capital of the JV company. The Singapore consortium's contribution to the registered capital will be in the form of cash (Lye and Chen 2010: 76–77). The Singapore consortium, the Singapore Tianjin Eco-City Investment Holdings (STEC), is currently wholly owned by Keppel Corporation. Keppel, however, is seeking international institutional investors to co-invest in STEC. Already, the Qatar Investment Authority has entered into an MOU with Keppel to accept Keppel's invitation to participate as an equity investor in the project by taking up a 10 percent stake in STEC (Keppel Corporation press release 2008).

The Chinese consortium, the Tianjin Eco-City Investment and Development Company (TEC), is led by the Tianjin TEDA Investment Holding Company. The Tianjin TEDA Investment Holding Company is wholly owned by the Tianjin municipal government. The company has spearheaded the development of the Tianjin Economic and Technological Development Zone (TEDA) since 1984. The company is also involved in various sectors such as property, finance, transport, and energy in the TBNA (with a total land area of 2,270 km^2) where both TEDA and the China-Singapore Tianjin Eco-city are located. The Tianjin TEDA Investment Holding Company therefore brings to the JV company not only valuable experience and expertise but also a strong network for conducting business. Most recently, the JV company signed on its first business partner when an MOU was signed in January 2009 with Sembawang Engineers and Construction Pte Ltd to work on the feasibility study for the development of a US$1 billion solar polysilicon production plant in the China-Singapore Tianjin Eco-city. Sembawang will be the project sponsor and developer of the plant and will lead a consortium of private investors to fund the development (Keppel Corporation press release 2009).

The China-Singapore Tianjin Eco-city aims to be environmentally friendly, socially harmonious, and economically sustainable. It is located in the Coastal Leisure and Tourism Zone of the TBNA. In terms of the time-line, the target is to complete the 3 km^2 start-up area by 2013. The entire development is expected to be completed in 10 to 15 years' time, with a projected population of 350,000 residents (Singapore's Ministry of National Development press release 2008c).

A major feature of the eco-city lies in its conversion of otherwise unproductive land to good use, where ecological rehabilitation is balanced with urban development. The eco-city will be built on a 30 km^2 site consisting largely of non-arable land, including salt farms and vacant land. There will be a central core (known as the eco-core) of conserved ecological wetlands and rehabilitated water bodies, including a wastewater pond currently being used as an effluent discharge ground. The areas surrounding the eco-core will be divided into four main districts, each to be served by an urban sub-center. Each district will have a mixture of residential, commercial, industrial, cultural, and recreational land.

The second key feature of the eco-city is the focus on maximizing convenience for residents by locating the necessary services and facilities nearby. The basic building block of the eco-city is the eco-cell that integrates different land uses within a modular 400 × 400 m grid. Educational institutions, commercial areas, workplaces, and recreational areas are distributed within these eco-cells, which are in turn sited within walking or cycling distance of residential areas. Together, the eco-cells form neighborhoods, districts and, eventually, urban centers.

The main mode of transport will be a light railway running through the eco-city. This will be complemented by cycle paths and green corridors. There will also be a secondary network of buses or trams. The goal is to make commuting via public transport and non-motorized means so convenient that residents will gradually rely less on, or even relinquish, the use of fossil-fueled vehicles. Certain incentives may also be introduced to achieve this goal (*Lianhe Zaobao* 2008). This approach takes into account current realities relating to individual preferences for owning private cars as a status symbol.

The third distinguishing feature of the eco-city is its strong message of social harmony or, more specifically, its efforts to meet the needs of ordinary people. The eco-city has positioned itself as a model of harmonious living where people from all walks of life, regardless of their income or social status, can come together. This is akin to Singapore's concept of neighborhood communities where different ethnic groups, professions, and religions can coexist as a vibrant and cohesive entity. In particular, about 20 percent of the residential areas in the eco-city will be set aside for public, subsidized housing (*First Financial Daily* 2008). To meet this goal, Singapore and China aim to draw on their experience of providing public housing and devise the most feasible way forward. It remains to be seen how this will be realized.

Related to the goal of social harmony is the resettlement of a group of about 2,000 villagers that would be affected by the development of the eco-city. Elsewhere in China, there have been numerous instances of resettlement cases gone awry, leading to affected residents protesting against the developers and local authorities. Given the sensitivity of resettlement cases, the Singapore and Chinese sides have taken particular care to address the concerns and needs of the potentially affected residents. It has been reported that the 2,000 villagers who need to relocate will be guaranteed jobs and housing in the eco-city (*The Straits Times* 2008). Meticulous handling of this issue will generate good publicity for the eco-city and strengthen its position as a place suitable for people from all walks of life.

A final attractive feature of the eco-city is the emphasis on putting into practice the best practices from the Singapore and Chinese sides. Each side appears willing to share and learn from the other. The collaboration can be described as a partnership rather than a one-way street with one side telling the other side how things should be done. By jointly contributing, the parties involved will have a greater vested interest in seeing the ideas come to fruition. For instance, the green area per person in the eco-city is set at 12 m^2 by 2013. In terms of water quality, the target is to make all water in the eco-city potable. All buildings in the eco-city will conform to green building standards that will marry Singapore's green mark with China's green standards. On transportation, the target is to achieve at least 90 per cent of residents walking, using public transport, or cycling when commuting within the eco-city by 2020. Another target is to have 100 per cent barrier-free access for residents in the eco-city. In terms of economic contribution, the target is to have at least 50 R&D scientists and engineers per 10,000 workforce in the eco-city by 2020, and at least 50 per cent of the employable residents in the eco-city should be employed in the eco-city by 2013 (Singapore's Tianjin Eco-city Office 2009) .

China's Ministry of Housing and Urban-Rural Development announced, on 6 April 2011, the results of the 2011 National Green Building Innovation Award. The Wan Tuo Residential Project (First Phase) in the Start-Up Area of the China-Singapore Tianjin Eco-city clinched the third class award. It was ranked 11 out of a total of 16 nationwide projects. On 29 March 2011, the Pan Asian Water Manufacturing (Tianjin) Co. Ltd (PAW) became the first investor in the Tianjin Eco-city Eco-Industrial Park (EIP). A groundbreaking ceremony was held for the construction of PAW's China headquarters and its key manufacturing base in the EIP. With this base, PAW will consolidate its existing manufacturing operations in China. The base will also serve as PAW's global logistics and warehousing hub, R&D center and control center for brand building, and marketing for Duvalco products. The total investment is 100 million yuan. On the same day, the topping out for Phase I of the Ready-Built Factories (RBFs) in the EIP took place. SSTEC will invest 220 million yuan for the construction of RBF Phase I with a built-up area of 63,800 m^2, to cater for a range of high-value, low-carbon footprint clean-tech production and other value-added operations. This green industrial space will provide manufacturing companies with a cost-effective and convenient platform to jump-start their business in the eco-city.

Over the years, the two governments of China and Singapore have been instrumental in identifying new projects which will allow them to stay relevant to each other's development needs, providing various platforms for political and economic engagement, and proactively addressing any issues that arise. Suzhou Industrial Park and Tianjin Eco-city underscore the determination of the two countries to add substance to their relationship. While differences may arise from time to time in carrying out various projects, both sides have accumulated experience in managing such differences. In fact, by working through differences together, each side can foster better understanding of the other, and this will create a more realistic basis for both countries to move forward. Seen in this light, the China-Singapore Tianjin Eco-city project is very important. If successful, it will provide further evidence that Singapore's experience in economic and environmental management is still relevant and valuable to China.

8 Emerging civil society in China's climate politics

In the past three decades, a string of structural changes, most prominently economic reform, opening-up, and decentralization, have created new windows of opportunity for citizen participation in the party-state of China where the policy-making process is being increasingly influenced by emerging non-governmental organizations (NGOs), mass media, on-line groups, and opinion leaders outside the bureaucratic system. The burgeoning civil society, albeit strictly restricted by the authoritarian regime, is able to exert a perceptible impact upon China's climate politics, in which internalization of norms and agenda setting are essential for the final policy outcome. Differing from the pressuring approaches often taken by their foreign peers to convey dissatisfaction and concerns, Chinese civic organizations tend to undertake peaceful activities that do not challenge governmental positions on the climate change issue, and thus do not jeopardize their own legal existence in China's political context. Even so, with the help of new information and communication technologies (ICTs) and linking-up with international environmental organizations, the role of NGOs and other civic forces as advocates of social norms and independent watchdogs in China's climate policy process should not be underestimated, as promotion of information sharing and public consciousness may be equally effective in reinforcing the climate position of an emerging economy within a restricted civil society.

The development of environmental NGOs in China

When the Chinese government started to deepen its reform and opening-up policy in the 1990s, civil activities became frequent and all kinds of NGOs working for public and special interests mushroomed. The interaction between the international advocacy networks/epistemic community and Chinese officials/scientists has not only fostered the government's shift to a proactive role in international environmental negotiations, but also stimulated the emergence of indigenous environmental NGOs (ENGOs) in China. Many exchange programs and conferences sponsored by international NGOs or scientific institutions took place in the 1990s when China was experiencing the "phase of tactical concessions" in climate negotiations (Schroeder 2008: 512). During this period, the World Wide

Fund for Nature (WWF) organized an international seminar on global warming in China; representatives of China's State Science Commission cooperated with the UN Centre for Science and Technology Development (Johnston 1998: 571); and the Climate Institute coordinated a meeting between Chinese and foreign scientists (CSCPRC *et al.* 1992: 190). With increasing awareness about environmental protection, people set up ENGOs engaged in environmental education, nature conservation, species protection, and policy advocacy among many other activities. The establishment of Friends of Nature in 1994 kicked off the rapid growth of ENGOs in China. Such organizations – a symbol of China's emerging civil society – have become a major source of environmental knowledge as well as champions of public participation in environmental protection. Although ENGOs have become increasingly visible players in China's green politics, their roles and functions are still quite restrained under China's current state-centric political systems and, therefore, they are not as powerful and influential as their international peers. Past experiences in Western countries since the 1960s show that significant supervision and participation from NGOs, the media, and other civil society groups are prerequisites for better environmental governance. So if China wants to address the ecological problem more efficiently, it has to improve the institutional environment for the vibrant growth of ENGOs and effective media surveillance. Meanwhile, in interaction with the traditional mass media, the internet and international NGOs, indigenous ENGOs can serve as both sites and agents of democratic social change in China (Yang 2005: 46). Friends of Nature, China's first ENGO, was established in 1994 when only nine ENGOs had been founded in China, including four student organizations. By 1996, the number had grown to 28, including ten student organizations. The number increased dramatically from 1997 to 1999, when at least 69 ENGOs were founded, 43 of which were student organizations (Yang 2005: 50). China's official statistics showed that, by the end of 2005, there were a total of 2,768 ENGOs in the country, with 224,000 employees, 69,000 of whom were full-time and 155,000 part-time (*Xinhua News* 2006). A total of 2.977 billion yuan (US$425 million) were raised by these 2,768 NGOs in 2005, and the numbers of ENGOs and their employees are expected by the All-China Environment Federation, a national ENGO with strong government backgrounds, to grow by 10–15 percent annually in China (*China Daily Online* 2006).

Generally speaking, China's ENGOs can now be categorized into seven types: registered NGOs, non-profit enterprises, unregistered voluntary groups, web-based groups, student environmental associations, university research centers and government-organized NGOs (GONGOs). In the state-centered country, GONGOs definitely enjoy far more financial advantage and policy convenience compared to other NGOs, but this kind of government background also restrains its role as a third force against the state and market. The large number of national and local environmental GONGOs, to some extent, represents the government's endeavor and willingness to fight against pollution. Due to administrative restraint and focus on academic activities, environmental GONGOs lack motivation and incentives to push forward environmental protection on certain sensitive issues. Compared to other ENGOs in China, however, some of these GONGOs, such as the China Association of the Environmental Protection Industry, the China Society of Environmental Sciences, the China Energy Conservation Association, and the Chinese Society for Sustainable Development, are more professional and boast expertise in environmental planning, decision making, enforcement ability and project application. Some of the incumbent or retired officials become heads of these GONGOs, and their efficient communication channels with other government departments facilitate routine activities in promoting environmental protection causes. Pan Yue, Vice Minister of the State Environmental Protection Administration, predecessor of the Ministry of Environmental Protection, acted as the leader of the China Environmental Culture Promotion Association (CECPA) for a long time. Pan, an outspoken official well-known for his criticism of China's environmental management system, used his influence in officialdom to make the CECPA play an active and sometimes aggressive role in semi-civil activities, which produced positive social impacts. The main activities of this association include training universities' environmental protection associations to enhance capacity building, holding forums on environmental protection, and promoting communication and interaction with grassroots organizations. In April 2005, CECPA developed an environmental training program in association with the Global Village of Beijing and the State Environmental Protection Administration (Fu 2007: 300).

Other kinds of ENGOs in China, which share a common aim of promoting environmental consciousness and public participation, avoid confrontational methods and adopt approaches that encourage learning, cooperation, and participation. Normal activities include public lectures, symposiums, field trips, newsletter announcements, on-line discussions, and even internet petitions. Although some organizations are edging their way into more contentious areas, the general tendency has been to shy away from radical issues and tactics.

While avoiding confrontational tactics, ENGOs in China often adopt the boundary-spanning strategy, which takes advantage of political grey areas to advance contestable claims and extract concessions and often "employs the rhetoric and commitments of the powerful to curb political or economic power" (O'Brien 2003: 53). Under China's authoritarian regime, ENGOs sometimes have to use the government's own words such as "sustainable development" and "environmental protection" as a weapon of protest, resistance, and collective actions. Legal action is a common practice by ENGOs to protect pollution victims and fight polluting industries.

China's ENGOs started their mission by means of environmental enlightenment education, and later became increasingly involved in concrete environmental protection, green community development, legal assistance, and exchanges with other NGOs. Friends of Nature was the first ENGO to introduce the mobile van for environmental education in China. Their van, named Antelope, traveled across urban and rural areas to popularize participatory environmental education in primary and middle schools (Fu 2007: 301). In 1999, the Global Village of Beijing took a refuse classification and sorting initiative to develop the concept of a green

Table 8.1 Main types of ENGOs in China

Organization type	*Registration status*	*Examples*
Registered NGOs	Registered as social organizations (*shehui tuanti*) or private, nonprofit work units (*minban fei qiye danwei*)	Friends of Nature; Green River
Nonprofit enterprises	Registered as business enterprises but operate as nonprofit organizations	Global Village of Beijing; Institute of Environment and Development
Unregistered voluntary groups	Unregistered organizations that function as NGOs	Green Earth Volunteers
Web-based groups	Unregistered groups that operate mainly through the internet	Green-Web; Greener Beijing
Student environmental associations	Registered with campus Youth Leagues yet function and perceived as NGOs	Sichuan University Environmental Volunteer Association
University research centers/ institutes	Affiliated with institutions of higher learning but operate as NGOs	Center for Legal Assistance to Pollution Victims, China University of Political Science and Law
Government-organized NGOs (GONGOs)	Social organizations established by government agencies, also known as state-owned NGOs (SONGOs)	China Environmental Science Association

Source: Yang (2005: 50).

community. After the year 2000, more and more ENGOs started to use the internet as a useful weapon to bypass the government's media censorship and impose pressure on some sensitive ecological issues. In 2003, more than ten ENGOs launched a joint advocacy effort to ask the government to reconsider the possible negative ecological effect of the South-to-North Water Diversion Project.

ENGOs' influence on climate policy

China currently does not have an indigenous NGO solely dedicated to climate protection, but many NGOs run climate-related campaigns (Schroeder 2008: 513). Some international networks specializing in climate change mitigation, including the Climate Action Network (CAN) and the Climate Group, have set up branches in China to spur local people into action against climate change. At the start of the millennium, NGOs framed their activities as energy-saving campaigns, because the issue of climate change was still considered by the government to be a sensitive political issue (Schroeder 2008: 517). Since China's ratification of the Kyoto Protocol in August 2002, an official indicator marking the internalization of mitigation and adaptation norms, ENGOs have been increasingly engaged in climate-related activities. During to the serious power shortage in the summer of 2004, the Global Village of Beijing and five other domestic and international ENGOs introduced, for the first time, a joint on-line initiative in Beijing, calling for the air-conditioned temperature in hotels, restaurants, and offices to be kept at 26° C for the sake of both energy saving and climate protection. With a mission to discuss and respond to climate issues and reach consensus on future actions regarding climate change, the Chinese Civilian Society on Climate Change Team was established in 2007, consisting of seven Chinese ENGOs, including Friends of Nature, the Global Village of Beijing, Green Earth Volunteers, the Institute of Public and Environmental Affairs, Greenpeace, Oxfam, and Action Aid. After rounds of consultations, seminars, and workshops, the Chinese Civilian Society on Climate Change Team in the same year publicized *A Warming China: Thoughts and Actions for the Chinese Civil Society*, a report that summarized the perspectives and positions of various governments and civil society groups around the world in international climate negotiation and attempted to establish a common perspective for Chinese civil society on this topic (Friends of Nature *et al.* 2007: 3). Yet, if people read the final page of the report that lays out the five positions suggested for adoption by Chinese civil society, it is not difficult to find that such core initiatives as "tackling climate change under UNFCCC" and "differentiated responsibilities between developed countries and developing countries" (Friends of Nature *et al.* 2007: 19) strongly resemble the Chinese government's persistent stance on the climate change issue. The report did urge the Chinese government to encourage and ensure the participation of civil society in the climate change policy-making process and implementation monitoring process, and to participate more proactively in international climate talks, but it failed to give detailed suggestions that might help to achieve these goals. Two years later, these seven NGOs published another joint document, *Chinese Civil Society on Climate Change 2009*, on the eve of the Copenhagen Climate Summit, to express their expectation of the birth of a post-Kyoto protocol during the forthcoming conference (Friends of Nature *et al.* 2009). This document went one step further by urging China to "set a good example" for all developing countries in tackling climate change, but it continued to repeat the Chinese government's basic position that developed countries should take the lead to cut emissions and transfer technology and funding to developing countries.

Chinese NGOs' limited role in pressuring the government to take on more aggressive mitigation responsibilities can be largely attributed to the unique "symbiotic situation" (Ho 2007: 198) between governmental organizations and indigenously registered NGOs that need governmental support for their daily operations. The borderline between NGOs and government-organized NGOs (GONGOs) is blurred because, according to the law, all NGOs to be established in China must have a sponsoring governmental institution before being registered to the Ministry of Civil Affairs. In such a semi-authoritarian context, NGO leaders and politicians are mutually dependent, and the Chinese government considers the actions of its domestic NGOs as acceptable only so long as these are in line with, or actually supporting, official policies, such as a public education campaign on energy-saving behavior (Schroeder 2008: 515). Investigation has shown that NGOs in China rated media and information-sharing campaigns as the best way to make their positions heard by policy makers, and they all agreed that Western NGO-style naming-and-shaming strategies were not an option; instead, they preferred to make awards to local governments which have made progress in energy saving (Schroeder 2008: 520).

Greening of media and internet

The Chinese media have been strong supporters of ENGOs from the outset, partly due to the "greening" of the media (Wen 1998: 39–44). Many media professionals directly participate in ENGOs as their organizers or members. Green Camp, Green Earth Volunteers, Green Plateau, the Tibetan Antelope Information Center, Tianjin Friends of Green, and Panjin Black-Beaked Gull Protection Association are all led by journalists or former journalists, while Friends of Nature counts some influential journalists among its members (Yang 2005: 56). Due to insufficient support from the government and market resources, some NGOs regard the media as powerful amplifiers of their voices. As environmental issues are often controversial and may easily raise eyebrows, the media like to put these events in the headlines and this is exactly what ENGOs want. In interaction with these ENGOs, some journalists get more involved in the environmental movement and become sympathetic to and supportive of green causes. Internationally speaking, the alliance between the media and ENGOs is quite common, but in China, with its special political system, journalists and reporters are in an awkward position, sandwiched between the Party superiors, who have political authority over the press, and the market, which places economic constraints on it (Liu 1998: 37). Thus, the media share structurally similar positions with ENGOs, and such structural homology fosters a reciprocal relationship between the media and ENGOs (Yang 2005: 56).

The media coverage and public controversies surrounding dam building on the Nu River, and its potentially dire ecological consequences, showed how effective the media could be in helping ENGOs to alter the government's agenda. According to incomplete statistics, from August 2003 to September 2004, this controversial issue became the focus of more than a hundred articles and campaigns by many influential newspapers, magazines, radio, and television outlets. The message in these reports grew increasingly critical, as they changed from positive comments to dissenting opinions, as revelations about the negative impacts of the dam surfaced (Fu 2007: 295). Diverse reporting perspectives and heated debates in the mass media helped public opinion to influence government policies. Some professional reporters renounced their role as independent and objective observers and became sympathizers for disadvantaged people and marginalized NGOs. Finally, in April 2004, China's State Council halted the hydropower project being planned on the Nu River in Yunnan Province. China's

Premier Wen Jiabao, reportedly cited "a high level of social concern" as an important reason for suspending the dam-building project. Such a reversal after public criticism has hardly been typical of the Chinese government – nor was the nature of the public criticism typical (Yang and Calhoun 2007: 211).

Compared with traditional media, the internet has the advantages of speed, broad reach, and interactivity. The number of Chinese internet users has been growing rapidly since the year 2000. In the first half of 2002, the number of netizens in China reached 45.8 million, jumping more than 30 percent in half a year. By the end of 2007, about 210 million Chinese people had become internet users, very close to the number of 215 million netizens in the United States. The year 2008 witnessed China boast the world's largest number of internet users, with a substantial number of rural people having access to the internet. Despite political controls and government censorship, Chinese internet users still find it more and more convenient to resort to the internet for public expression and political activism, especially against a backdrop of severe restriction of the traditional media.

Now most ENGOs in China have their own websites. The internet provides the platform to share information and knowledge, and some ENGOs maintain active mailing lists that send environmental information regularly to subscribers by email. The internet is being used by individual ENGOs to expand their capacity and engage in dialogues with other interest groups. When the voices from some marginalized organizations are amplified by the internet, they tend to attract more social attention and have a larger influence on policy-making process. Currently, information exchanges between NGOs through e-forums and e-newsletters are becoming increasingly frequent, and joint advocacy targeting focal issues demonstrates the intensive interaction among NGOs (Fu 2007: 296). Many ENGO websites also have bulletin boards for public discussion, and blogs have become a new on-line way for individuals to express their views, release news, and publicize pictures and videos concerning environmental issues. Together with the rapid growth of both the number and influence of ENGO websites, more and more environmental activists are creating personal homepages on the internet. The internet's networked nature facilitates and accelerates information spread among numerous websites, including both related environmental websites and non-relevant ones. When just one or two ENGO websites or personal homepages start to discuss certain environmental issues, these issues are likely to spread quickly to other websites and even enter the limelight of traditional media like newspapers and television.

Besides the internet, other modern telecommunication means such as short-messages (SMS) through mobile phones can also provide non-traditional channels for information circulation on sensitive environmental issues. With increasing public awareness of environmental issues, local people will sometimes voluntarily join collective actions to safeguard legitimate rights that might be threatened by possible pollution. In May and June 2007, several hundred people staged a peaceful demonstration against a planned chemical plant named Tenglong Aromatic PX Co. in southern China's Xiamen City. The work was suspended by the government after residents sent about 1 million mobile phone SMS in protest about possible health dangers (AP News 2007b).

Political constraints and challenges facing Chinese ENGOs

The Chinese government has to some extent encouraged the development of NGOs for handling increasing social problems. Chinese high-level officials have praised ENGOs such as Friends of Nature and called for support for the healthy development of these organizations. The government promulgated two regulations in 1998 to provide a regulative framework for the registration and management of NGOs and non-profit organizations. These regulations have had both positive and negative impact upon the development of NGOs in China.

On the one hand, they represent official recognition of the legal status of such organizations. On the other hand, they also contain very restraining articles. According to the regulations, any social organization to be established in China has to have a sponsoring governmental institution before being registered with the Ministry of Civil Affairs. This presents a major hurdle to registration because an NGO is considered a liability not an asset to its sponsoring institution (Jin 2001: 5–8). Besides, the regulations stipulate that, in the same administrative area, there should not be more than one organization for any specific area of work (such as environmental protection). In many cases, GONGOs have already filled that fixed quota (Yang 2005: 55). Even Liu Qi, a member of the Chinese Communist Party Politburo and Party Secretary of Beijing, complained in March 2008 that such compulsory linkage between the government and social organizations has hampered the normal development of social organizations (Southern Metropolitan News 2008). Figures show the number of NGOs per 10,000 citizens is 110 in France, 97 in Japan and only 2.1 in China, while the total expenditure on China's NGOs only accounts for less than 1 percent of its GDP, much lower than world's average of 4.6 percent and developed countries' average of 7 percent (China.com.cn 2006).

Moreover, due to the government's strict control of and restrictions on NGOs, it is difficult for NGOs to recruit enough capable personnel. It is also not easy for most NGOs to obtain funding from private or state-owned Chinese companies. Many ENGOs have to resort to foreign foundations, international ENGOs and multinational corporations. In many instances this practice increases the government's distrust of some ENGOs, raising the suspicion that such funding from overseas sources may mask political intentions to subvert the government. As most ENGOs in China cannot raise funds in the same way as their foreign peers, many face a problem of financial shortage that hampers their normal operation and routine activities.

Although most Chinese ENGOs have become increasingly mature and sophisticated after more than a decade of development, they still face insufficiency and weakness in their managerial structure and professional capacity, which prevents them from playing a larger role in boosting social environmental protection causes. Despite the growing public environmental concern in China, the actual environmental knowledge of Chinese citizens is still quite limited, which inhibits the further development of ENGOs.

Many of China's first generation of grassroots ENGOs are informal in management and function, and depend too much on their founder-leader. Leaders' personal ambitions and charisma shaped these organizations and mobilized followers. Management was not institutionalized and decision making remained concentrated among a small group of individuals (Fu 2007: 307). These ENGOs need to institutionalize their managerial structure and improve internal evaluation systems to promote administrative efficiency. As today's environmental problems become more and more sophisticated, the solutions to these problems demand expertise in environmental engineering, chemistry, medical knowledge, biology, meteorology, and other sciences. For example, the controversial and high-profile issue of climate change is a multi-disciplinary problem that not only involves natural sciences, but also relates to social sciences including economics, political science, international relations, and sociology. Lack of professional knowledge in these areas will prevent these organizations from playing an active and effective role in influencing governmental decision making and setting public agendas. Under such circumstances, ENGOs need to adopt a professional rather than a general perspective to cope with certain environmental issues. In order to have a more in-depth understanding of issues raised at public hearings on environmental impact, present evidence more effectively and work with administrative and bureaucratic systems more successfully, ENGOs have to raise their professional levels and enhance their capacity building. The Environmental Impact Assessment (EIA) report on the Nu River is a case in point. The report, containing more than 700 pages, touched on various branches of science, so it is an urgent task for NGO experts to translate the content of the report into scientifically sound and convincing proposals that will lead to professional environmental decision making (Fu 2007: 308). The time for relying on a charismatic leader has passed and there is an urgent need for Chinese ENGOs to standardize their operational and managerial procedures and increase their professional standards. Without a favorable policy condition in China, however, it is very difficult for NGOs to attract funds as well as talented professionals. The de facto restrictions from the government, therefore, have an indirect influence upon the capacity building of ENGOs in China. Despite the large number of ENGOs in the country, they can actually only play very limited roles in supervising the government and setting agendas. The insufficient development of ENGOs hampers China's ability to fight against pollution.

The gap between Chinese and international ENGOs is still significantly large in terms of management structures and professional standards. Unlike many international NGOs that enjoy transnational influence and strong expert support, Chinese ENGOs are not experienced in the international arena and therefore their perspectives are relatively limited and their actions seldom encompass a global outlook.

Furthermore, international ENGOs are more diversified and many of them have special interest areas, such as climate change, water pollution, biodiversity protection, acid rain prevention, and animal rights protection. In comparison,

Chinese ENGOs tend to be more homogeneous. It is easier for many Chinese ENGOs to find problems and file complaints than to provide solutions. Chinese ENGOs have been expanding exchanges and cooperation with their international counterparts, but the lack of English-speaking staff has prevented many of them from making frequent contact with international NGOs or actively participating in international talks and forums. Now more and more international negotiations on certain environmental issues invite transnational and indigenous ENGOs to participate, while some international forums and dialogue platforms are first initiated or dominated by these ENGOs. However, on many of these occasions, it is difficult to find a deep involvement of Chinese NGOs, whose voices are not often heard in the international arena. Chinese ENGOs still need more support from the government as well as their own endeavors to change their previous charismatic-leader style of operation to a more teamwork-based model, with increased participation in international dialogues and activities.

9 Conclusion: motivations behind policy consistencies and variations

With a mix of authoritarian politics and a quasi-liberalized market economy, China's climate change policy process is fragmented, profit-driven and self-defensive, seemingly leaving little room for significant compromises or changes. Yet, in response to rising international pressures and domestic energy security issues, the regime has demonstrated some flexibility and shrewdness in coping with the newly emerged challenges. Whereas international pressure has not been able to change China's stance of no legally binding commitments, China is trying to transform such external pressure into a rare opportunity to upgrade and optimize its economic and industrial structure, an effort that progresses slowly in the face of strong resistance. With the focus still on economic growth and employment, the government, through tapping business potential in the green sector, is trying to make environmental protection policy an accelerator rather than a brake to the sizzling economy. China's history records how formidable dynasties were overthrown by uprisings caused by climate disasters, but it is not evident that current Chinese climate-related policies have been motivated primarily by concern about vulnerability to global climate change, which is still seen by the government as a peripheral issue. China's policy making on climate change is more likely driven by its intense attention to energy security, business opportunities in emerging green industries and its international image in global climate politics.

Environmental concern as a vehicle to pursue development

Although China's official statements have claimed that the "climate in China has experienced noticeable changes over the past 100 years," which may cause a certain negative impact upon its "vulnerable ecosystem" (NDRC 2007: 4 and 14), this vast continental state, with most of its territory located in the temperate zone, is less vulnerable to climate change consequences than many other developing countries, especially those located in tropical or littoral regions. Studies (WHO 2003; Confalonieri *et al.* 2007; Maplecroft 2010) have revealed that the actual and virtual vulnerability to climate change depends on various factors and future projections, that include the economic development level, food availability, population density, geographical position and quality, and the availability of public health-care provision. There are many examples that showed correlation with climate change and large uncertainties and exhibit considerable variation across regions. Vulnerability to climate change varies due to economic development and geographical position (i.e. variations of summer conditions and monsoons), and demographic subgroups but, overall, the most affected groups are children, elderly people, indigenous populations, chronically ill people, people with a low income, and coastal communities (Lemmen and Warren 2004; Ebi *et al.* 2006; Confalonieri *et al.* 2007). Less developed nations located in tropical and littoral areas with few natural resources and limited infrastructures are particularly vulnerable. According to the Climate Change Vulnerability Index (CCVI) that evaluates national vulnerabilities based on exposure to climate-related natural disasters and sea-level rise, human sensitivity in terms of population patterns, development, natural resources, agricultural dependency and conflicts, and adaptive capacity of a country's government and infrastructure to combat climate change, China only ranked 49th in the world and was put in the "high risk" category instead of the "extreme risk" category where India and Thailand featured (Maplecroft 2010). Although China is perceived to be more vulnerable to climate change than most industrialized nations, the continental state with its massive hinterland in the temperate zone, well-established infrastructure, and enhanced economic capacity is in a better position than most developing nations to adapt to climate change. However, in contrast to Russia and the United States, two landmass colossuses that are notorious for their indifference to mitigation actions, China has been gradually drifting from its previous position of suspicion about climate consequences to firmer stances that support emissions reduction and adaptation actions on a global scale. Albeit China has not significantly changed its insistence on the "common but differentiated responsibilities" and still refuses to accept legally binding emissions cutting obligations, the Chinese government has been making greater efforts to promote public awareness about climate change and to formulate more aggressive policies and targets in the realm. The year 2007 became a watershed when China for the first time publicized its "National Climate Change Program," which went even further than the IPCC's assessment report by claiming that China's air temperature rise during the past 100 years was slightly greater than the average global temperature rise (NDRC 2007: 4). In the same year, after Chinese delegates were besieged by environmental activists, protesting against the country's rapidly-growing carbon emissions, in the Bangkok conference held by IPCC, the ruling Chinese Communist Party for the first time included the notion of "conservation culture" (*shengtai wenming*) in its political report in which emission and energy issues, once under the shadow of economic targets and marginalized in China's top-level decision-making process, became new policy focuses (Chen 2009a: 144). Since then, a series of new stringent policies and programs and economic incentives and disincentives, as well as institutional changes have been launched to encourage low-carbon activities and curb energy guzzlers with high carbon emissions.

Warning that "the nationwide annual mean air temperature would increase by 1.3–2.1° C in 2020 and 2.3–3.3° C in 2050 as compared with that in 2000,"

China's "National Climate Change Program" projected a grim picture under the business-as-usual scenario, saying that future climate change may lead to a decline in agricultural output, aggravation of desertification, shrinking of grassland area, glaciers and frozen earth, loss of biodiversity, expansion of arid areas, further rise of sea level along the Chinese coast, a surge in typhoons and storms, and increased frequency and intensity of the heat waves that may cause more deaths and serious diseases (NDRC 2007: 5 and 16–19). Nevertheless, China's unique inter-agency bureaucratic structure on climate policy making, as well as the consistencies and variations identified in its climate-related policy formulation, has revealed that increasing awareness of potential climate consequences can only partially explain China's shift towards more aggressive mitigation actions. As a developing country that has always put economic growth ahead of environmental protection, China has for years been authorizing the NDRC, the economic planning and energy regulation agency, and the Ministry of Foreign Affairs to take charge of climate-related policy making, instead of other more environmentally conscious departments like the Ministry of Environmental Protection and the China Meteorological Administration. The establishment of the National Leading Group to Address Energy Saving, Emission Cutting and Climate Change in 2007 even reinforced such development-dominant mechanism rather than weakening it, because Premier Wen Jiabao, whose top priority was national economic growth and employment, took the top position in the Leading Group while Vice Premier Zeng Peiyan, ex-NDRC commissioner and State Councilor Tang Jiaxuan, ex-Foreign Minister, became his two assistants. NDRC's interest in climate change is to a large extent related to its long-standing concern about China's energy scarcity that may put a brake upon its economic growth and the industrial upgrading that may enhance competitiveness and create more jobs. China's windfall from the lucrative carbon business through the Clean Development Mechanism has also fuelled NDRC's attention to low-carbon industry, which is booming as one of the major business opportunities of the twenty-first century. China's great leap forward in sharpening its competitive edge on those low-carbon sectors is a natural extension of the country's preferred "no-regret" strategy that emphasizes mitigation actions providing fringe benefits like profitability and employment, regardless of whether the threat of climate change is real. The NDRC wishes to utilize climate change as a moral driving force to boost clean energy and other green sectors so as to serve the dual goals of cleaning up and finding new growth points for its economy in the aftershock of the global financial crisis.

As for the Ministry of Foreign Affairs, its principal concerns in international climate negotiations are always the protection of state sovereignty (especially the right to develop its own national economy without external interference) and the enhancement of China's international image. Neither of these two administrations that dominate China's climate policy making have any inherent institutional interests in caring about the potential ecological consequences of climate change in the long run, so the principal motivations driving China's climate policy formulation are the considerable fringe benefits linked with high-profile affirmative policy statements and selective emission-cutting actions in practice. After China realized that the mitigation of climate change had gradually become the widely acknowledged norm accepted by the mainstream of the international community, its policy makers decided to stand with the majority instead of challenging the consensus. Studies have shown that, since the late 1970s, even on such contentious issues as human rights that often irk China, the rising power has moved closer to internationally accepted standards rather than openly objecting to them (Kent 1999; Foot 2000; Chen 2009b).

External epistemic influence through multi-channeled international interactions cannot be ignored during the internalization of these norms in China but, unfortunately, those Chinese institutions – including their officials and scientists – that interacted the most with the international advocacy networks/epistemic community have been marginalized in the later climate policy-making process when the top leadership realized that climate change is a vital issue that may put economic growth, international image, and even employment and foreign trade at stake. The Chinese government's perception of climate change has been clearly stated in the Foreword of China's National Climate change Program as "it [climate change] is an issue involving both environment and development, but is ultimately an issue of development" (NDRC 2007). Hence it is not difficult to understand why the Chinese government has been increasingly keen on aggressive mitigation targets and actions that could push forward its sluggish economic and industrial restructuring process along the low-carbon and service-oriented path while still being reluctant to shoulder legally binding obligations. The same logic applies to the explanation of the real motives behind China's great leap forward in developing clean energy, electric cars. and other environmental industries, which has been mainly driven by the ambition to sharpen competitive edge in the newly emerging green businesses rather than by any sense of responsibility for the mitigation of global climate change. Solar water heating (SWH) systems have been widely used in China's vast rural areas since the early 1980s, when the climate change issue was unknown to most Chinese households. As the world's largest market for solar thermal applications and the largest producer of solar heat collectors, China's popularization of SWH is mostly the result of the country's poverty alleviation and energy-saving effort in rural and township areas rather than growing climate change consciousness. China's fervor in producing polysilicon, an important industrial raw material necessary for the development of the solar energy industry, is another example proving that economic motives rather than climate/environment consciousnesses are the fundamental driving forces behind most of China's ambitious green initiatives. Although the wide use of solar panels is an important way to reduce human dependence upon carbon-intensive fossil fuels, the manufacturing process of polysilicon guzzles energy and produces highly toxic byproducts that pollute the surrounding environment and can render the land barren. Lured by the hefty profits in the lucrative but highly polluting business, a large number of polysilicon projects all over the country were permitted by the Chinese government between 2007 to 2009 to start manufacturing polysilicon on massive scales. It was not until early 2011 that the government decided to suspend polysilicon project approval, after realizing that projected overcapacity and high energy consumption were threatening the industry's profitability. The case explicitly demonstrated that the real motive behind China's ambitious low-carbon initiatives, as well as its active participation in the CDM, is commercial profit rather than concern about climate change, which is still seen as a peripheral issue by the country's policy makers.

Amid increasing global concerns about climate change, resource scarcity, and other pollution problems, the low-carbon and environmental industries are booming as major business opportunities in the twenty-first century. Facing mounting environmental problems across the country and growing civic pressures, China's ambitious plan to boost the environment industry as a strategic pillar industry could serve the dual goals of cleaning up and finding new growth points for its economy in the aftershock of the global financial crisis. When China unveiled its four-trillion yuan stimulus package in November 2008 to boost the economy during the global financial crisis, a total of 210 billion yuan or 5.25 percent of the stimulus money was earmarked for environmental protection projects and improving energy efficiency. China's determination to become the global leader in green industry goes beyond a mere response to the ecological challenges brought by pollution, and has much to do with jobs and profits. As a sunrise industry, the rapidly growing energy-saving and environmental protection sectors that manufacture sustainable products and transfer green technologies are said to be more resilient to the economic downturn than their counterparts in traditional industry. The major socio-economic challenges faced by the Chinese government are those of creating sufficient job opportunities and maintaining stellar economic growth in the near future. Having claimed the mantle of being the world's factory, China is trying to secure its position as one of the world's major manufacturing bases for ad hoc green products, and thus absorb excess labor from other overcapacity industries.

Climate policy: a part of China's energy strategy

China's climate strategy remains centered on its energy development strategy as driven by its overall economic development goals (Lewis 2007: 155). The government has been viewing the close relationship between climate change and fossil fuel utilization more from an energy security perspective rather than from an emissions perspective. In other words, the Chinese government, when facing various policy options on mitigation actions, usually prioritizes measures that can promote new energy and energy efficiency for the sake of safeguarding energy supply instead of those that purely serve the purpose of emissions reduction. As the NDRC, the country's major energy regulator, is the dominant player in its domestic process on climate policy, China's climate policy has gradually and inevitably become a part of its overall energy strategy whose fundamental goal is to ensure continued economic growth and prosperity for its people. Energy consumption is still seen as the key to economic development and is the main factor that prevents the Chinese government from taking on quantified emission reduction commitments. China's climate policy is determined by a string of domestic and international considerations such as economic growth, energy security, perceived vulnerability, sovereignty, and international image, but among all factors, the regime's preoccupation with meeting the voracious demand for energy arising from the swelling economy has set the tone of its climate policy. Therefore, understanding the background for energy policy making can always help us to reach a better understanding of a crucial determinant of China's climate policy. Cheap energy has engendered rapid economic growth, reduced poverty, and raised living standards in China and, as the economy develops and living standards rise, its demand for energy rises correspondingly quickly (Heggelund 2007: 161–62). China's refusal to accept any legally binding emission-cutting obligations throughout the UNFCCC climate negotiations is closely linked with its energy-sufficiency and development-first strategy that inherently lacks flexibility in such a gigantic developing nation. The ad hoc climate change inter-agency system dominated by the NDRC, the pro-development energy regulator, is thereby the natural result of an institutional arrangement deliberately designed by the top leadership whose priority is economy and energy. By enhancing the advantageous positions of domestic energy giants, while weakening the role of environmental organizations, such entrenched policy making has further consolidated China's pro-development stance in international climate talks.

The party-state, which has perceived economic growth, poverty alleviation, and social stability as the foundation of its legitimacy, has not changed the standpoint that emission-reduction commitments, by imposing a ceiling upon national energy consumption, will restrict the economy and employment. Nevertheless, landmark events like the implementation of the Kyoto Protocol and the global financial crisis in the past decade have, in fact, softened China's rigid stance on the issue when the largest emerging economy came to realize that mitigation actions (like CDM projects and renewable energy development) also offer vital economic potential that provides enormous business opportunities and should not be ignored. The international price hike in coal and crude oil, which has been closely linked with the rise of emerging markets, especially China and India, has made the Chinese government realize that its overdependence upon fossil-based energy, and coal in particular, will not be sustainable. The Chinese government now has the perception that if addressed properly, the climate change concern, instead of infringing China's right to meet its energy demand and develop its economy, could be a god-given tool to facilitate the country in diversifying energy supply, finding new economic growth points, and enhancing international competitiveness. Therefore, it is not difficult to understand why, although the Chinese government is insistent on non-binding commitments in international negotiations, the regime has established attractive energy/carbon intensity targets from time to time and input billions of dollars to boost renewable energy industries and develop low-carbon zones.

China's future stance in post-Bali negotiations

The Fourth Assessment Report (AR4), released by the Intergovernmental Panel on Climate Change in 2007, made the connection between climate change and human activity with a high degree of certainty. The Kyoto Protocol, which is scheduled to expire in 2012, cannot meet the demand from the international community for further emission reductions. At the UN climate change summit in Bali (Indonesia), December 2007, a new round of international negotiations was formally introduced to work out a new accord to replace the Kyoto Protocol. In the post-Bali talks, environmental activists are hoping the United States, along with China and India, will be included in the new treaty with quantitative emission quotas or even a comprehensive carbon tax. China is in a dilemma. On the one hand, it is fretting about reputational damage precipitated by its deteriorating environmental problem and rapidly growing emissions, banking on international cooperation to solve it; on the other hand, it fears that emission abatement obligations may inhibit its fast economic growth. In future talks, it is still very unlikely that China will yield to international pressure and accept mandatory emission-cutting targets, but it will probably use voluntary carbon-intensive benchmarks as substitutions for cap-and-tax obligations. Moreover, China will participate more frequently in other bilateral and multilateral diplomatic activities on climate change, aside from the UN-track climate talks, to polish its international image and alleviate external pressures.

Voluntary targets instead of compulsory obligations

Regarding compulsory emission targets as a cap on domestic economic growth, Chinese officials have, on many occasions, articulated the country's adherence to the policy of "common but differentiated responsibilities" and objected to any legal responsibility on quantifiable reductions. From China's perspective, international effort against climate change is a double-edged sword; while a positive outcome in terms of funding and technology transfer to China, it makes a wholly different and negative impact if shackles are placed upon the giant through a disadvantageous pact arising from future negotiations. Chinese experts argue that, if China accepts emission quotas similar to those of the industrialized nations in the Kyoto Protocol, the cost will outweigh any current gains derived from CDM projects to buy emission permits from other countries at a higher carbon price in the post-Kyoto period. The alternative carbon tax, if adopted in the next protocol, is expected to cost the Chinese industry billions of dollars at a conservative estimate – given that China's economy and emission continue to grow at current rates.

China's negotiation tactic is clear: utilize voluntary carbon-intensity-based targets based on the reduction of energy consumption or emissions per unit of economic output to replace mandatory emission cuts and ease international pressures. As climate change engenders imminent and foreseeable disastrous consequences, such moderate goals cannot satisfy many environmentalists and negotiating parties. The European Union passed a new Energy Plan in March 2007, requesting China, India, and the United States to sanction a more ambitious plan to cut GHG emissions.

Acknowledging the international pressure for its compulsory emissions reduction, the Chinese government is trying to play a low-profile role in the global carbon trade. In February 2007, several reports surfaced intimating that Beijing hoped to establish an exchange for trading carbon emissions permits to capitalize on China's emergence as a hotspot in the multi-billion dollar carbon market. China's Office of the National Coordination Committee on Climate Change posted a statement on its website that stated the contrary. The short statement read, "currently the Chinese government has no plan to establish a so-called 'Climate Exchange'" adding that, under the Kyoto Protocol, such emissions trading schemes could only be set up in countries with binding targets (China's Office of the National Coordination Committee on Climate Change 2007).

Continued solidarity with developing countries

More than 100 developing countries have been acting collectively since the early days of the global climate negotiations to strengthen their voices and fend off pressures from industrialized nations. Although huge political, economic, and geographic disparities have always existed among Third World nations, they nonetheless formed the "G-77 plus China" bloc to build a common purpose and safeguard the collective interest when negotiating with affluent Western countries. Despite its large size and special status in the UN Security Council, China has preferred to ally itself with G-77 to deal with the complicated and new topic of climate change that was first proposed by the industrialized world. In the post-Kyoto negotiation that was officially launched during the Bali conference, China will continue to reinforce strategic solidarity with the Third World rather than deviate from the bloc and act alone. In fact, China's alliance with the G-77 has not waned, and its willingness to "go-it-alone" has declined even further.

China's desire to stay inside the bloc, however, is facing more challenges due to some members' willingness to break ranks; while others are complaining about the unequal distribution of CDM profits among developing countries. Some Latin American countries, led by Brazil and Argentina, have shown an eagerness to accept similar quantitative emission obligations to those of Western countries, while China and India fear legally binding goals will hamper their burgeoning industrialization process. Small island countries that are more vulnerable to climate change are expressing their dissatisfaction about responsibility shirking by major emitters, while petroleum-exporting nations such as Saudi Arabia stand as strong objectors to the international climate regime.

Meanwhile, the imbalance of CDM income distribution, as well as China's surging energy consumption and emissions, have led to many developing countries' discontent about the current climate change regime dominated by the Kyoto Protocol. Many developing countries, including mostly poorer nations vulnerable to global warming, have been largely left out of the wealth-sharing of CDM projects. In 2006, the whole of Africa received less than US$150 million from the sale of carbon credits from CDM projects, or 3 percent of the global total. With foreign exchange reserves of more than US$1.7 trillion, China is no longer a poor member of the Third World. Whether other developing countries will still regard China as one of their own and continue the close alliance is questionable.

More attention to regional mechanisms

As the UN-track (or Kyoto-track) climate change regime features quantifiable emission cutting targets, China is planning to join more regional mechanisms on climate change that emphasize non-compulsory energy-efficiency programs. While China still claims that global climate talks should be conducted within the framework of the United Nations, in practice it has become more active than before in joining all types of bilateral and multilateral cooperation mechanisms against climate change – outside the purview of the UN-track.

Multilaterally, China is more willing to accept international agreements that call for voluntary actions rather than those with mandatory emissions-cutting targets. This will undoubtedly assist China to enhance its soft power while protecting its hard power (economic growth). In 2005, China made common cause with Australia, India, Japan, South Korea, and the United States to establish the Asia-Pacific Partnership on Clean Development and Climate, which emphasized energy conservation and technology cooperation in lieu of setting mandatory emissions-cutting targets. The United States and Australia, two of its members, refused to ratify the Kyoto Protocol at that time. The Asia-Pacific Partnership on Clean Development and Climate is a cooperation mechanism outside the UNFCCC and Kyoto Protocol; as a member, China obtains advanced energy-efficiency technology from affluent countries, coordinates diplomatic positions with other heavyweights in international climate talks, and improves its international image in the green area without accepting legally binging targets. In recent years, many existing multilateral organizations, including APEC (Asia-Pacific Economic Cooperation), ASEAN (Association of Southeast Asian Nations) Plus Three (China, Republic of Korea, and Japan), and G-8, have started to augment special mechanisms on climate change. Subsequently, China has proved to be an active participant or dialogist in forums, conferences, and cooperation programs held by these mechanisms. During the September 2007 APEC summit in Sydney, both China and the United States accepted a program with non-binding goals on energy efficiency and afforestation. According to the program, APEC members need to reduce energy intensity by 25 percent by 2030, and to increase forest cover in the region by at least 20 million hectares by 2020.

Bilaterally, China is attentive to cooperative programs on clean energy and emission reduction with industrialized nations, including the United States. Climate change has become an indispensable area of interest within China's recent bilateral talks with many Western countries. China also embraces bilateral coordination and cooperation with India and other developing powers on the climate issue. During the Indian Prime Minister Manmohan Singh's visit to China in January 2008, climate change was also on the agenda and the two sides reached consensus that neither China nor India should be obligated to make commitments to reduce carbon emissions.

China will definitely face greater challengers and pressures in the coming climate talks. China's economic strength has grown so rapidly in the past decade that the international community expect it to shoulder greater international responsibilities on climate change. While it is unduly problematic for China to accept legally binding targets for emission reductions, state leaders understand very clearly that its soft power will be greatly damaged if it continues to pursue conventional means. China will try to gain more support and sympathy from both developed and developing countries through frequent diplomatic exchanges and will work to reduce domestic carbon emissions per GDP unit continuously and, remarkably, will seek to fulfill zero carbon growth by the middle of this century. China would need to rethink the current tactics if the United States were to reverse its position and take on an emission- reduction commitment. Predictably, even under this scenario, China's development-first mindset and inter-agency bureaucracy would still make legally binding obligations unacceptable.

Bibliography

Online articles for which a Chinese translation of the title is given in brackets are available on the internet in Chinese only.

AFP News (2007) "Question marks over China's climate commitment," 6 May 2007.

Andrews-Speed, C.P. (2004) *Energy Policy and Regulation in the People's Republic of China*, The Hague: Kluwer Law International.

AP News (2007a) "China rejects climate mandates, blames lavish U.S. for crisis," available at: www.usatoday.com/weather/climate/2007-12-07-bali-climate-conference_N.htm (accessed January 2012).

AP News (2007b) "Protests against Xiamen chemical plant continue despite decision to suspend," available at: http://english.sina.com/china/1/2007/0601/113774.html (accessed January 2012).

Araujo, Joao Lizardo de, Rosa, Luiz Pinguelli and Silva, Neilton Fidelis da (2009) "Hydroelectricity: Future Potential and Barriers," in *Generating Electricity in a Carbon-constrained World*, edited by Fereidoon Perry Sioshansi, Oxford: Academic.

AsiaTimes Online (2009) "China leads solar home revolution," available at: www.atimes.com/atimes/China_Business/KJ29Cb02.html (accessed January 2012).

BBC News online (2010) "China rejects Mekong River dam criticism," available at: http://news.bbc.co.uk/2/hi/8603112.stm (accessed January 2012).

Bloomberg News online (2007) "Carbon-credit sales may double this year," available at: www.climos.com/news/articles/carboncreditsales.htm (accessed January 2012).

Bloomberg News online (2010) "China's Tianjin may be first APEC low-carbon city," available at: www.bloomberg.com/apps/news?pid=20601130%20&sid=a6VpM8mFEYyw (accessed January 2012).

Bo, Zhiyue (2010) "China's new National Energy Commission: Policy implications," Singapore: *EAI* (East Asian Institute) *Background Brief*, No. 504.

Bradsher, Keith (2010) "China leading global race to make clean energy," *New York Times Online*, available at: www.nytimes.com/2010/01/31/business/energy-environment/31renew.html (accessed January 2012).

Chandler, William and Wang, Yanjia (2009) "Memo to Copenhagen: Commentary is misinformed – China's commitment is significant," web commentary from Carnegie Endowment for International Peace. Available at: www.carnegieendowment.org/files/Memo_to_Copenhagen_edits_Revised_12-14-091.pdf (accessed January 2012).

Chen, Gang (2008) "China's diplomacy on climate change," in *The Journal of East Asian Affairs*, Vol. 22, No. 21, 145–74.

Chen, Gang (2009a) *Politics of China's Environmental Protection: Problems and Progress*, Singapore: World Scientific.

Chen, Dingding (2009b) "China's participation in the international human rights regime: A state identity perspective," *Chinese Journal of International Politics*, Vol. 2, pp. 399–419.

China Business News (*diyi caijing ribao*) (2008) "Sino-Singapore Tianjin Eco-City Master Plan is released, in year 2020 the population will reach 350,000" (*Zhongxin Tianjin shengtaicheng zongti fangan chulu, 2020 nian jiangda 35 wanren*), available at: http://city.finance.sina.com.cn/city/2008-05-07/99740.html (accessed January 2012).

China.com.cn (2006) "China's environmental protection at the crossroad" (*shizilukou de zhongguo huanjing baohu*), available at: www.china.com.cn/chinese/zhuanti/hjwj/1161880.htm (accessed January 2012).

China Daily Online (2006) "Rocky road to a brighter environment," available at: http://china.org.cn/english/environment/173598.htm (accessed January 2012).

China Daily Online (2009a) "Wind power gets set for huge thrust," available at: www.chinadaily.com.cn/business/2009-06/03/content_7966752.htm (accessed January 2012).

China Daily Online (2009b) "Nuclear power goal revised to 86GW," available at: www.chinadaily.com.cn/bizchina/2009-07/02/content_8345808.htm (accessed January 2012).

China Daily Online (2010) "TEDA strives for energy efficiency with international help," available at: www.chinadaily.com.cn/cndy/2010-04/12/content_9713945.htm (accessed January 2012).

China Daily Online (2011) "China to prioritize hydropower," available at: www.chinadaily.com.cn/business/2011-06/23/content_12763475.htm (accessed January 2012).

China Electricity Council (2010) "Statistical brief on China's electricity industry" (*quanguo dianli gongye tongji kuaibao 2010*), available at: http://tj.cec.org.cn/tongji/niandushuju/2011-02-23/44236.html (accessed January 2012).

China Energy News (*zhongguo nengyuan bao*) (2010) "*The potential and prospect of China's uranium resources*" (*Zhongguo you ziyuan de qianli yu qianjing*), 5 July, p. 19.

China Meteorological Administration (CMA) (2010) "New progress made in surveying China's wind power resources" (*woguo fengneng ziyuan xiangcha he pingjia qude xinjinzhan*), online, available at: www.cma.gov.cn/mtjj/201001/t20100104_55673.html (accessed January 2012).

China National Offshore Oil Corporation (CNOOC) press release (2010) "Premier Wen Jiabao Visits Tianjin Lishen Battery Co., Ltd.," available at: http://en.cnooc.com.cn/data/html/news/2010-05-14/english/301361.html (accessed January 2012).

China National Petroleum Corporation (CNPC) press release (2008) "Tianjin climate exchange unveiled," available at: www.cnpc.com.cn/eng/press/newsreleases/CSR/d1495066-3c79-482a-a36b-88b834cf3f78.htm (accessed January 2012).

China's Office of the National Coordination Committee on Climate Change (2007) "Comment on the Report about setting up a climate exchange in China," available at: http://cdm.ccchina.gov.cn/web/main.asp?ColumnId=25 (accessed January 2012).

cn.WSJ.com (*Wall Street Journal* online edition in Chinese) (2010) "On-grid preferential pricing policy to push forward China's solar power industry" (*shangwang dianjia youhui zhengce jiangzhutui zhongguo taiyangneng chanye*), available at: http://chinese.wsj.com/gb/20100429/ffe140657.asp (accessed January 2012).

Committee on Scholarly Communication with the People's Republic of China (CSCPRC) *et al.* (1992), *China and Global Change: Opportunities for Collaboration*, Washington, DC: National Academy Press.

Confalonieri, U., Menne, B., Akhtar, R., Ebi, K.L., Hauengue, M., Kovats, R.S., Revich, B. and Woodward, A. (2007) "Human health climate change 2007: Impacts, adaptation and vulnerability," in Parry, M.L., Canziani, O.F., Palutikof, J.P., Linden, P.J. van der and Hanson, C.E. (eds), *Fourth Assessment Report of the Intergovernmental Panel on Climate Change*, pp. 391–431, Cambridge: Cambridge University Press.

Dasgupta, C. (1994) "The climate change negotiations," in Irving M. Mintzer, J. Amber Leonard (eds) *Negotiating Climate Change: The Inside Story of the Rio Convention*, Cambridge: Cambridge University Press, pp. 129–48.

Downs, Erica S. (2008) "China's 'new' energy administration," *China Business Review*, November–December 2008, pp. 42–45.

Ebi, K.L., Smith, J., Burton, I. and Scheraga, J.S. (2006) "Some lessons learned from public health on the process of adaptation," *Mitigation and Adaptation Strategies for Global Change*, 11, pp. 607–20.

Economy, Elizabeth C. (1997) "Chinese policy-making and global climate change: two-front diplomacy and the international community," in Miranda A. Schreurs and Elizabeth C. Economy (eds) *The Internationalization of Environmental Protection*, Cambridge: Cambridge University Press, pp. 19–41.

Economy, Elizabeth C. (1998) "China's environmental diplomacy", in Samuel S. Kim (ed.) *China and the World: Chinese Foreign Policy faces the New Millennium* (4th edition), Boulder: Westview Press, pp. 264–83.

Ecoworld (2008) "Wind power in China," online, available at: www.ecoworld.com/energy-fuels/wind-power-in-china.html (accessed January 2012).

Ellerman, A. Denny, Jacoby, Henry D. and Decaux, Annelène (1998) *The Effects on Developing Countries of the Kyoto Protocol and CO_2 Emission Trading*, World Bank publication.

First Financial Daily (2008) "Sino-Singapore Tianjin Eco-city Master Plan Released" (*Zhongxin Tianjin Shengtaicheng Zongti Fangan Chulu*), 7 May.

Foot, Rosemary (2000) *Rights Beyond Borders: The Global Community and the Struggle over Human Rights in China*, Oxford: Oxford University Press.

Forbes (2009) "Weaknesses in Chinese wind power," available at: www.forbes.com/2009/07/20/china-wind-power-business-energy-china.html (accessed January 2012).

Friends of Nature *et al.* (2007) *A Warming China: Thoughts and Actions for the Chinese Civil Society*, available at: http://www.oxfam.org.hk/content/98/content_3529en.pdf (accessed January 2012).

Friends of Nature *et al.* (2009) *Chinese Civil Society on Climate Change 2009* (*2009 zhongguo gongminshehui yingdui qihoubianhua lichang*), available at: www.ipcc.cma.gov.cn/Website/index.php?ChannelID=13&NewsID=909 (accessed January 2012).

Fu, Tao (2007) "Development of environmental NGOs in China," in Liang Congjie and Yang Dongping (eds), *The China Environment Yearbook 2005: Crisis and Breakthrough of China's Environment*, Boston: Brill.

Gaffron, Philine, Huismans, Ge and Skala, Franz (2008) *Ecocity Book II: How to Make it Happen*, Vienna: Facultas Verlags- und Buchhandels AG.

Global Wind Energy Council (2011) "Global wind report: Annual market update 2010," online, available at: www.gwec.net/fileadmin/images/Publications/GWEC_annual_market_update_2010_-_2nd_edition_April_2011.pdf (accessed January 2012).

Greenpeace (2009) "China's carbon intensity target not enough," online, available at: www.greenpeace.org/eastasia/news/china-carbon-intensity (accessed January 2012).

Guardian (2009) "How do I know China wrecked the Copenhagen deal? I was in the room," online, available at: www.guardian.co.uk/environment/2009/dec/22/copenhagen-climate-change-mark-lynas (accessed January 2012).

Guardian (2011) "China warns of 'urgent problems' facing Three Gorges dam," online, available at: www.guardian.co.uk/world/2011/may/20/three-gorges-dam-china-warning (accessed January 2012).

Hao, Yufan and Lin, Su (eds) (2005) *China's Foreign Policy Making: Societal Force and Chinese American Policy*, Burlington: Ashgate.

Hardin, Garrett (1968) "The tragedy of the commons," *Science*, Vol. 162, No. 3859, pp. 1243–48.

Hatch, Michael (2003) "Chinese politics, energy policy, and the international climate change negotiations" in *Global Warming and East Asia: The Domestic and International Politics of Climate Change*, Paul G. Harris (ed.), London: Routledge, pp. 43–65.

Heggelund, Gorild (2007) "China's climate change policy: Domestic and international developments," *Asian Perspective*, Vol. 31, No. 2, pp. 155–91.

Ho, Peter (2007) "Embedded activism and political change in a semiauthoritarian context," *China Information*, Vol. 21, No. 2, pp. 187–209.

Hoffmann, Matthew J. (2005) *Ozone Depletion and Climate Change: Constructing a Global Response*, Albany: State University of New York Press.

ifeng.com news (2011) "China's path of developing hydropower" (*shuidian fazhan de zhongguo lujing*), available at: http://finance.ifeng.com/news/industry/20110519/4044549.shtml (accessed January 2012).

Intergovernmental Panel on Climate Change (IPCC) (2007) "Summary for policymakers" in *Climate Change 2007: Mitigation. Contribution of Working Group III to the Fourth Assessment Report of the Intergovernmental Panel on Climate Change*, B. Metz, O.R. Davidson, P.R. Bosch, R. Dave and L.A. Meyer (eds), Cambridge: Cambridge University Press.

International Energy Agency (IEA) (2006) "Key world energy statistics 2006," online, available at: www.iea.org/textbase/nppdf/free/2006/key2006.pdf (accessed January 2012).

International Energy Agency (IEA) (2007) "World Energy Outlook 2007 executive summary: China and India insights," online, available at: www.iea.org/Textbase/npsum/WEO2007SUM.pdf (accessed January 2012).

International Herald Tribune (2007) "China knows which way wind blows – Country gets largest share of UN credits to curb emissions," 10 May, p. 1.

Jahiel, Abigail R. (1998) "The organization of environmental protection in China," in Edmonds, Richard Louis (ed.), *Managing The Chinese Environment*, Oxford: Oxford University Press.

Jin, Jiaman (2001) "The growing importance of public participation in China's environmental movement," in Jennifer Turner and Fengshi Wu (eds), *Green NGO and Environmental Journalist Forum: A Meeting of Environmentalists in Mainland China, Hong Kong, and Taiwan*, Washington, DC: The Woodrow Wilson Center, pp. 5–8.

Johnston, Alastair I. (1998) "China and international environmental institutions: A decision rule analysis" in Michael B. McElroy, Chris P. Nielson and Peter Lydon (eds) *Energizing China: Reconciling Environmental Protection and Economic Growth*, Cambridge, MA: Harvard University Center for the Environment.

Kent, Ann (1999) *China, the United Nations, and Human Rights: The Limits of Compliance*, Philadelphia: University of Pennsylvania Press.

Keohane, Robert O. (1998) "International institutions: Can interdependence work?" *Foreign Policy*, Issue 110: pp. 82–96.

Keppel Corporation press release (2008) "Sino-Singapore Tianjin Eco-city," available at: www.kepcorp.com/en/content.aspx?sid=97 (accessed January 2012).

Keppel Corporation press release (2009) "Sino-Singapore Tianjin Eco-city Signs MOU with First Business Partner for US$1 Billion Project," available at: www.kepcorp.com/en/news_item.aspx?sid=1946 (accessed January 2012).

Kobayashi, Yuka (2003) "Navigating between 'luxury' and 'survival' emissions," in *Global Warming and East Asia: The Domestic and International Politics of Climate Change*, Paul G. Harris (ed.), London: Routledge, pp. 86–108.

Lampton, David (ed.) (2001) *The Making of Chinese Foreign and Security Policy in the Era of Reform 1979–2000*, Stanford, CA: Stanford University Press.

Lemmen, D.S. and Warren, F.J. (eds) (2004) *Climate Change Impacts and Adaptation: A Canadian Perspective*, Government of Canada report.

Lewis, Joanna (2007) "China's strategic priorities in international climate change negotiations," *The Washington Quarterly*, Vol. 31, No. 1, pp. 155–74.

Li, Lei (2010) "Brief analysis of current China's PV industry: Part II" (*woguo guangfuchanye fazhanxianzhuang jianxi zhier*), in *Solar & Renewable Energy Sources* (*yangguang nengyuan*), Vol. 2, 2010, pp. 36–39.

Li, Ling (2007) "China Urges Electricity Suppliers to Buy 'Green' Power," online posting, available at: http://www.renewableenergyworld.com/rea/news/article/2007/09/china-urges-electricity-suppliers-to-buy-green-power-49879 (accessed January 2012).

Lianhe Zaobao (2008) "Sino-Singapore Joint Venture Company Established, Tianjin Eco-City Moves from Master Planning into Real Combat" (*Zhongxin hezi gongsi chengli, Tianjin shengtaicheng cong guihua jinru shizhan*), available at: www.zaobao.com.sg/special/singapore/pages4/sg_cn080702.shtml (accessed January 2012).

Lieberthal, K.G. (1992) "Introduction: The 'fragmented authoritarianism' model and its limitations," in K.G. Lieberthal and D.M. Lampton (eds) *Bureaucracy, Politics, and Decision Making in Post-Mao China*, Berkeley, CA: University of California Press, 1–30.

Lieberthal, K.G. and Oksenberg, M. (1988) *Policy Making in China: Leaders, Structures and Processes*, Princeton, NJ: Princeton University Press.

Liu, Hong (1998) "Profit or ideology? The Chinese press between Party and market," *Media, Culture & Society*, No. 20.

Lo, Carlos Wing-Hung and Tang, Shui-Yan (2007) "Institutional reform, economic changes, and local environmental management in China: The case of Guangdong Province" in Neil T. Carter and Arthur P.J. Mol (eds), *Environmental Governance in China*, London: Routledge.

Lu, Xuedu and Liu Deshun (eds) (2004) *Clean Development Mechanism in China: Taking a Proactive and Sustainable Approach*, Beijing: Tsinghua University Publishing House.

Lye, Liang Fook and Chen, Gang (eds) (2010) *Towards a Livable and Sustainable Urban Environment: Eco-cities in East Asia*, Singapore: World Scientific.

Ma, Xiaoying and Ortolano, Leonard, (2000) *Environmental Regulation in China: Institutions, Enforcement, and Compliance*, Oxford: Rowman & Littlefield Publishers.

McGregor, Richard (2007) "China more assertive in climate talks," *Financial Times Online*, available at: http://www.ft.com/intl/cms/s/0/86073606-fa59-11db-8bd0-000b5df10621.html#axzz1jIqqd8lH (accessed January 2012).

Maplecroft (2010) "Big economies of the future – Bangladesh, India, Philippines, Vietnam and Pakistan – most at risk from climate change," available at: http://maplecroft.com/about/news/ccvi.html (accessed January 2012).

Miller, Ronald and Blair, Peter (1985) *Input-Output Analysis: Foundations and Extensions*, Englewood Cliffs, NJ: Prentice-Hall.

National Bureau of Statistics of China (2010) *China Statistical Yearbook 2010*, Beijing: China Statistics Press.

National Development and Reform Commission (NDRC) (2005) *Measures for Operation and Management of CDM Projects in China*, Beijing, online, available at http://cdm.ccchina.gov.cn/english/NewsInfo.asp?NewsId=905 (accessed January 2012).

National Development and Reform Commission (NDRC) (2007) "China's National Climate Change Programme," online, available at: www.ccchina.gov.cn/WebSite/CCChina/UpFile/File188.pdf (accessed January 2012).

National Development and Reform Commission (NDRC) (2008) "China Renewable Energy Development Overview 2008," online, available at: www.cresp.org.cn/uploadfiles/7/977/2008en.pdf (accessed January 2012).

National Development and Reform Commission (NDRC) (2009a) "Implementation of the Bali Roadmap: China's Position on the Copenhagen Climate Change Conference," online posting, available at: http://en.ndrc.gov.cn/newsrelease/t20090521_280382.htm (accessed January 2012).

National Development and Reform Commission (NDRC) (2009b) "National On-grid Wind Power Tariff List" (*quanguo fenglifadian biaogan shangwang dianjiabiao*), online posting, available at: www.sdpc.gov.cn/zcfb/zcfbtz/2009tz/W020090727530432780298.pdf (accessed January 2012).

Nye, Joseph S. (2004) *Soft Power: The Means to Success in World Politics*, New York: Public Affairs.

O'Brien, Kevin J. (2003) "Neither transgressive nor contained: Boundary-spanning contention in China," *Mobilization*, Vol. 8, No. 1.

Office of the National Coordination Committee on Climate Change and Institute of Nuclear and New Energy Technology of Tsinghua University (2006) *Guidelines on China's CDM Project Development*, Beijing: China Environmental Science Publishing Company.

Olson, Mancur (1965) *The Logic of Collective Action: Public Goods and the Theory of Groups*, Cambridge, MA: Harvard University Press.

Organisation for Economic Co-operation and Development (OECD) (1999) *Action Against Climate Change: The Kyoto Protocol and Beyond*, Paris: OECD.

Oster, Shai (2007) "China scraps Green GDP report," *Wall Street Journal* (17 July 2007), p. A8.

Owen, Jerry (2011) "The Water Page: Yangtze River," online, available at: www.african-water.org/yangtze.htm (accessed January 2012).

Penn, Merlin (2007) "Coal production and balance of demand in China," online posting, available at: www.helium.com/items/763467-coal-production-and-balance-of-demand-in-china (accessed January 2012).

People's Daily Online (2007) "Lingbi: Overstaffing in the EPB and pollution fee not enough for making a living" (*Anhui lingbi, huanbaoju renmanweihuan, paiwufei bugou chifan*), available at: http://env.people.com.cn/GB/6049107.html (accessed January 2012).

People's Daily Online (2010a) "China launches low-carbon pilot in select cities, provinces," available at: http://english.peopledaily.com.cn/90001/90778/90862/7110049.html (accessed January 2012).

People's Daily Online (2010b) "ADB approves $135 mln loan for China's green power plant," available at: http://english.peopledaily.com.cn/90001/90778/90860/6890894.html (accessed January 2012).

PRC Amended Law on Conserving Energy (2007), online, available at: www.gov.cn/jrzg/2007-10/28/content_788493.htm (in Chinese) (accessed January 2012).

PRC Amended Law on Renewable Energy (2009), online, available at: www.npc.gov.cn/npc/xinwen/2009-12/26/content_1538199.htm (in Chinese) (accessed January 2012).

PRC Renewable Energy Law (2005), online, available at: www.renewableenergyworld.com/assets/download/China_RE_Law_05.doc (accessed January 2012).

Register, Richard (2002) *Ecocities: Building Cities in Balance with Nature*, Berkeley, CA: Berkeley Hills Books.

REN21 (Renewable Energy Policy Network for the 21st Century) (2009) *Recommendations for Improving the Effectiveness of Renewable Energy Policies in China*, online, available at: www.ren21.net/pdf/Recommendations_for_RE_Policies_in_China.pdf (accessed January 2012).

Reuters News (2009a) "China hands out $293 million subsidy for renewable power," available at: www.reuters.com/article/idUSTRE55O0JR20090625 (accessed January 2012).

Reuters News (2009b) "China offers big solar subsidy, shares up," available at: www.reuters.com/article/idUSPEK12570920090721 (accessed January 2012).

Reuters News (2009c) "China to subsidize purchases of clean-energy cars," available at: www.reuters.com/article/2009/01/27/us-china-cars-green-idUSTRE50Q0WQ20090127 (accessed January 2012).

Reuters News (2010) "U.S. could fall behind China in clean energy: Locke," available at: www.reuters.com/article/2010/05/22/us-china-usa-cleanenergy-idUSTRE64L0QD20100522 (accessed January 2012).

Reuters News (2011) "China freezes nuclear approvals after Japan crisis," available at: www.reuters.com/article/2011/03/16/us-china-nuclear-idUSTRE72D1PN20110316 (accessed January 2012).

Richerzhagen, Carmen and Scholz, Imme (2007) "China's capacities for mitigating climate change," *World Development*, Vol. 36, No. 2.

Rothwell, Geoffrey and Graber, Rob (2009) "The role of nuclear power in climate change mitigation," in *Generating Electricity in a Carbon-constrained World*, Fereidoon Perry Sioshansi (ed.), Oxford: Academic.

Schroeder, Miriam (2008) "The construction of China's climate politics: Transnational NGOs and the spiral model of international relations," *Cambridge Review of International Affairs*, Vol. 21, No. 4, December 2008, pp. 505–25.

Seligsohn, Deborah and Levin, Kelly (2010) "China's carbon intensity goal: A guide for the perplexed," *China FAQs*, online, available at: www.chinafaqs.org/files/chinainfo/ChinaFAQs_China's_Carbon_Intensity_Goal_A_Guide_for_the_Perplexed_0.pdf (accessed January 2012).

Shanghai Securities News (2006) "CDM deal worth 2 billion yuan hitting Juhua," 6 January 2006, p. A7.

Shirk, S.L. (1993) *The Political Logic of Economic Reform in China*, Berkeley, CA: University of California Press.

Shui, Bin and Harriss, Robert (2006) "The role of CO_2 embodiment in US–China trade," *Energy Policy*, 34, pp. 4063–68.

sina.com news (2010) "Tianjin Binhai New Area to invest 14 billion yuan in low-carbon industries," (*tianjin binhaixinqu 140yiyuan dazao ditanchanye jiqun*), available at: http://news.dichan.sina.com.cn/2010/05/13/160042.html (accessed January 2012).

sina.com news (2011) "Abolishment of wind power subsidy confirmed," (*fengdian butie queding beiquxiao*), available at: http://finance.sina.com.cn/chanjing/cyxw/20110618/141710012325.shtml (accessed January 2012).

Singapore's Ministry of National Development press release (2007) "Agreements to develop eco-city in China signed," available at: http://www.tianjinecocity.gov.sg/Press%20Releases/2007/11_18_2007.htm (accessed January 2012).

Singapore's Ministry of National Development press release (2008a) "First meeting of the Sino-Singapore Tianjin Eco-City Joint Working Committee in Tianjin," available at: www.tianjinecocity.gov.sg/Press%20Releases/2008/01_31_2008.htm (accessed January 2012).

Singapore's Ministry of National Development press release (2008b) "Inaugural Sino-Singapore Tianjin Eco-city Joint Steering Council meeting," available at: www.tianjinecocity.gov.sg/Press%20Releases/2008/09_03_2008.htm (accessed January 2012).

Singapore's Ministry of National Development press release (2008c) "Sino-Singapore Tianjin Eco-City draft master plan unveiled," available at: www.tianjinecocity.gov.sg/Press%20Releases/2008/04_17_2008.htm (accessed January 2012).

Singapore's Tianjin Eco-city Office (2009) "Key Performance Indicators of the Eco-city," available at: www.tianjinecocity.gov.sg/KPI.htm#21 (accessed January 2012).

Southern Metropolitan News (*Nanfang Dushi Bao*) (2008) "It's difficult to find 'mother-in-law': 20-year obstacle for NGOs" (*pojia nanzhao: minjian zuzhi qiujie ershinian zhikun*), 16 March 2008, p. A10.

Spencer, Richard (2007) "China rejects key EU climate change target," *Telegraph Online*, available at: www.telegraph.co.uk/news/worldnews/1553582/China-rejects-key-EU-climate-change-target.html (accessed January 2012).

Spiegel Online International (2010) "How China and India sabotaged the UN Climate Summit," available at: www.spiegel.de/international/world/0,1518,692861,00.html (accessed January 2012).

SSTEC (Sino-Singapore Tianjin Eco-City Investment and Development Co., Ltd.) (2010) "Tianjin Eco-City attracts 6 new investments in manufacturing and R&D, with a total investment amount of RMB 1 billion," available at: www.tianjineco-city.com/en/news_center/press_release/1117.aspx (accessed January 2012).

TEDA Investment Promotion Bureau (2010) "preferential policies on wind energy-related enterprises," available at: http://en.investteda.org/aboutteda/keyindustriesbrief/wind/default.htm#6 (accessed January 2012).

Telegraph (2009) "China and America to blame for Copenhagen failure, says Brown," available at: www.telegraph.co.uk/news/newstopics/politics/6859567/Gordon-Brown-Copenhagen-China.html (accessed January 2012).

The PEW Charitable Trusts (2010) *Who's Winning the Clean Energy Race?: Growth, Competition and Opportunity in the World's Largest Economies*, online, available at: www.pewtrusts.org/uploadedFiles/wwwpewtrustsorg/Reports/Global_warming/G-20%20Report.pdf?n=5939 (accessed January 2012).

The Straits Times (2007) "Singapore, China to jointly develop an 'Eco-City'," 26 April 2007, p. A10.

The Straits Times (2008) "$9.7b price tag for landmark Tianjin eco-city," 7 May 2008, p. A9.

Tianjin Daily (2009) "Binhai New Area: Low-carbon economy era is approaching" (*binhai xinqu: ditan jingji shidai jiasu daolai*), 12 August 2009, p. 11.

Tianjin Environmental Protection Bureau (2010) "Report on Tianjin's environmental situation in 2009" (*2009nian tianjinshi huanjing zhuangkuang gongbao*), available at: www.tjhb.gov.cn/tabid/182/InfoID/26962/Default.aspx (accessed January 2012).

Tianjin Municipal Government (2007) "Tianjin Municipal Master Plan (*tianjinshi chengshi zongti guihua*) (2005–2020)", available at: www.tj.gov.cn/tblm/ztbd/tbbd1/uppro/200710/t20071009_27983_2.htm (accessed January 2012).

UNEP (United Nations Environment Programme) press release (2007) "China closes ozone depleting chemical plants," online, available at: www.unep.org/documents.multilingual/default.asp?documentid=514&articleid=5624&l=en (accessed January 2012).

UNEP (United Nations Environment Programme), Cities Alliance & Local Governments for Sustainability (ICLEI) (2007). *Livable Cities: The Benefits of Urban Environmental Planning*. Washington DC, available at http: http://www.unep.org/urban_environment/PDFs/LiveableCities.pdf (accessed January 2012).

United Nations (1992) "United Nations Framework Convention on Climate Change" (UNFCCC), online, available at: http://unfccc.int/resource/docs/convkp/conveng.pdf (accessed January 2012).

United Nations (1999) *Handbook of Input-output Table Compilation and Analysis*, Studies in Methods Series F, No. 74, Handbook of National Accounting, New York: United Nations, online, available at: http://unstats.un.org/unsd/publication/SeriesF/SeriesF_74E.pdf (accessed January 2012).

United Nations Framework Convention on Climate Change (UNFCCC) (2011a) "Registered projects by host party," online available at: http://cdm.unfccc.int/Statistics/index.html (accessed January 2012).

United Nations Framework Convention on Climate Change (UNFCCC) (2011b) "Expected average annual CERs by host party," online, available at: http://cdm.unfccc.int/Statistics/index.html (accessed January 2012).

US Carbon Dioxide Information Analysis Center (2011a) "Preliminary 2008–09 global and national estimates," online, available at: http://cdiac.ornl.gov/ftp/trends/co2_emis/Preliminary_CO2_emissions_2009.xls (accessed January 2012).

US Carbon Dioxide Information Analysis Center (2011b) "People's Republic of China fossil-fuel CO_2 emissions: Trends," available at: http://cdiac.ornl.gov/trends/emis/tre_prc.html (accessed January 2012).

US Energy Information Administration (2008) "Metric tons of carbon dioxide per thousand (2000) U.S. dollars using market exchange rates," available at: www.eia.doe.gov/emeu/international/carbondioxide.html (accessed January 2012).

Wall Street Journal Online (2007) "China Scraps Green GDP Report," 17 July.

Watson, Jim and Wang, Tao (2007) "Is the west to blame for China's emissions?" *China Dialogue*, online posting, available at: www.chinadialogue.net/article/show/single/en/1592-Is-the-west-to-blame-for-China-s-emissions (accessed January 2012).

Weber, Christopher, Peters, Glen, Guan, Dabo and Hubacek, Klaus (2008) "The contribution of Chinese exports to climate change," *Energy Policy*, 36, pp. 3572–77.

Wen, Bo (1998) "Greening the Chinese media," *China Environment Series*, Issue 2, pp. 39–44.

WHO (World Health Organization) (2003) "Methods of assessing human health vulnerability and public health adaptation to climate change," in *Health and Global Environmental Change Series*, No. 1, Denmark: WHO Regional Office for Europe.

World Energy Council (2010) *2010 Survey of Energy Resources*, London: World Energy Council.

World Nuclear Association (2011a) "Nuclear power in China," online, available at: www.world-nuclear.org/info/inf63.html (accessed January 2012).

World Nuclear Association (2011b) "World nuclear power reactors and uranium requirements," available at: www.world-nuclear.org/info/reactors.html (accessed January 2012).

Xinhua News (2006) "Chinese environmental NGOs called on to play a bigger role," available at: http://news3.xinhuanet.com/english/2006-10/29/content_5261715.htm (accessed January 2012).

Xinhua News (2007) "China: Developing nations should set own emissions reduction targets," available at: http://news.xinhuanet.com/english/2007-11/23/content_7133154.htm (accessed January 2012).

Xinhua News (2010) "China starts up first fourth generation nuclear reactor," available at: http://news.xinhuanet.com/english2010/china/2010-07/22/c_13409085.htm (accessed January 2012).

Yang, Guobin (2005) "Environmental NGOs and institutional dynamics in China," *The China Quarterly*, No. 181, pp. 46–66.

Yang, Guobin and Calhoun, Craig (2007) "Media, civil society, and the rise of a green public sphere in China," *China Information*, Vol. 21 (2), pp. 211–36.

Yang, Mu and Pan, Rongfang (2010a) "China's wind power industry: From infant to growth stage," Singapore: *EAI (East Asian Institute) Background Brief*, No. 525.

Yang, Mu and Pan, Rongfang (2010b) "Harvesting sunlight: Solar photovoltaic industry in China," Singapore: *EAI (East Asian Institute) Background Brief*, No. 562.

Yang, Mu and Pan, Rongfang (2011) "Nuclear power industry in China," Singapore: *EAI Background Brief No. 593.*

Yu, Hongyuan (2008) *Global Warming and China's Environmental Diplomacy*, New York: Nova Science Publishers, Inc.

Zeenews (2010) "Brahmaputra Dam not aimed against India: China," online, available at: http://zeenews.india.com/news/nation/brahmaputra-dam-not-aimed-against-india-china_668559.html (accessed 17 November 2010).

Zhang, Guobao (2005) "How can energy shortage be blamed on China?" (*nengyuan jinzhang zenneng guaizui zhongguo*) *People's Daily Overseas Edition*, 21 September 2005, p. 1.

Zhang, Zhihong (2003) "The forces behind China's climate change policy," in *Global Warming and East Asia: The Domestic and International Politics of Climate Change*, Paul G. Harris (ed.), London: Routledge, pp. 66–85.

Zhao, Jimin (2002) "The multilateral fund and China's compliance with the Montreal Protocol," *Journal of Environment and Development*, Vol. 11, Issue 4, pp. 331–54.

Zhou, X. (1997) "Advantage of climate change to warm," *Beijing Review*, Vol. 40, Issue 23, 9–15 June, pp. 18–19.

Index

Note: page numbers in **bold** refer to illustrations.

Taylor & Francis

eBooks

FOR LIBRARIES

ORDER YOUR FREE 30 DAY INSTITUTIONAL TRIAL TODAY!

Over 23,000 eBook titles in the Humanities, Social Sciences, STM and Law from some of the world's leading imprints.

Choose from a range of subject packages or create your own!

Benefits for you

- Free MARC records
- COUNTER-compliant usage statistics
- Flexible purchase and pricing options

Benefits for your user

- Off-site, anytime access via Athens or referring URL
- Print or copy pages or chapters
- Full content search
- Bookmark, highlight and annotate text
- Access to thousands of pages of quality research at the click of a button

For more information, pricing enquiries or to order a free trial, contact your local online sales team.

UK and Rest of World: **online.sales@tandf.co.uk**

US, Canada and Latin America:
e-reference@taylorandfrancis.com

www.ebooksubscriptions.com

ALPSP Award for BEST eBOOK PUBLISHER 2009 Finalist

Taylor & Francis eBooks
Taylor & Francis Group

A flexible and dynamic resource for teaching, learning and research.

eupdates
Taylor & Francis Group

Want to stay one step ahead of your colleagues?

Sign up today to receive free up-to-date information on books, journals, conferences and other news within your chosen subject areas.

Visit
www.tandf.co.uk/eupdates
and register your email address, indicating your subject areas of interest.

You will be able to amend your details or unsubscribe at any time. We respect your privacy and will not disclose, sell or rent your email address to any outside company. If you have questions or concerns with any aspect of the eUpdates service, please email eupdates@tandf.co.uk or write to: eUpdates, Routledge, 2/4 Park Square, Milton Park, Abingdon, Oxfordshire OX14 4RN, UK.

Routledge Paperbacks Direct

Bringing you the cream of our hardback publishing at paperback prices

This exciting new initiative makes the best of our hardback publishing available in paperback format for authors and individual customers.

Routledge Paperbacks Direct is an ever-evolving programme with new titles being added regularly.

To take a look at the titles available, visit our website.

www.routledgepaperbacksdirect.com

Routledge
Taylor & Francis Group

ROUTLEDGE PAPERBACKS DIRECT

ROUTLEDGE
Revivals

Are there some elusive titles you've been searching for but thought you'd never be able to find?

Well this may be the end of your quest. We now offer a fantastic opportunity to discover past brilliance and purchase previously out of print and unavailable titles by some of the greatest academic scholars of the last 120 years.

Routledge Revivals is an exciting new programme whereby key titles from the distinguished and extensive backlists of the many acclaimed imprints associated with Routledge are re-issued.

The programme draws upon the backlists of Kegan Paul, Trench & Trubner, Routledge & Kegan Paul, Methuen, Allen & Unwin and Routledge itself.

Routledge Revivals spans the whole of the Humanities and Social Sciences, and includes works by scholars such as Emile Durkheim, Max Weber, Simone Weil and Martin Buber.

FOR MORE INFORMATION

Please email us at **reference@routledge.com** or visit:
www.routledge.com/books/series/Routledge_Revivals

www.routledge.com

Routledge
Taylor & Francis Group